GOOD·OLD·DAYS®

Country Roads™

© Away From It All by John Sloane

Edited by Ken and Janice Tate

HOUSE of
WHITE
BIRCHES
PUBLISHERS
SINCE 1947

Country Roads™

Editors: Ken and Janice Tate
Managing Editor: Barb Sprunger
Editorial Assistant: Joanne Neuenschwander
Copy Editors: Michelle Beck, Nicki Lehman, Läna Schurb
Assistant Editors: Marla Freeman, Marj Morgan, June Sprunger

Publishing Services Manager: Brenda Gallmeyer
Graphic Arts Supervisor: Ronda Bechinski
Cover Design/Production Artist: Erin Augsburger
Traffic Coordinator: Sandra Beres
Production Assistant: Janet Bowers, Chad Tate
Photography: Tammy Christian, Christena Green, Kelly Heydinger
Photography Assistant: Linda Quinlan
Photography Stylist: Tammy Nussbaum

Chief Executive Officer: John Robinson
Publishing Director: David McKee
Marketing Director: Shirrel Rhoades
Book Marketing Director: Craig Scott
Editorial Director: Vivian Rothe
Publishing Services Director: Brenda Wendling

Printed in the United States of America
First Printing: 2003
Library of Congress Number: 2002113545
ISBN: 1-59217-010-2

Good Old Days Customer Service: (800) 829-5865

Every effort has been made to ensure the accuracy of the material in this book.
However, the publisher is not responsible for research errors or typographical mistakes in this publication.

We would like to thank the following for the art prints used in this book.

For fine-art prints and more information on the artists featured in *Country Roads*, contact:

Curtis Publishing, Indianapolis, IN 46202, (317) 633-2070, www.curtispublishing.com
The Hadley Companies, Bloomington, MN 55438, (952) 943-8474, www.hadleylicensing.com
Newmark USA, Louisville, KY 40299, (502) 266-6752, www.newmarkusa.com
Bob Pettes, Parkville, MO 64152, (816) 587-1754
Norman Rockwell Family Trust, LaGrangeville, NY 12540, (845) 454-0859
John Sloane, Kirkland, IL 60146, (815) 522-6162

1 2 3 4 5 6 7 8 9

Dear Friends of the Good Old Days,

When I was a youngster, I often lamented growing up along country roads. They were dusty and gritty. I was hoping for a life filled with Hollywood adventure and glamour— but I found myself living scenes out of *The Grapes of Wrath.*

More than anything, I thought all country roads were naturally dead ends. The only way to escape the dead end, I thought, was to leave the country road behind.

The fact is, country roads have always taken me where I wanted to go.

They took me "over the river and through the woods" to Grandma's house, not only for holidays but also virtually every Sunday afternoon of my young life.

They took me to my Uncle Spencer's house for Saturday night music parties on warm summer nights. There we would sing and dance and Daddy and his brothers made music under the stars. Sometimes my cousin Gary and I walked down the country road that lined their property, talking in the moonlight about cars we would someday own, girls we would someday date, dreams we would someday realize.

It was a country road that led me to the love of my life. She was a fiery redhead named Janice who lived exactly three-quarters of a mile off the nearest pavement down a country lane with near neighbors as scarce as hen's teeth. Like the roads of our youth, courting in those days was a lot slower paced, but we found the pace suited us just fine. One year later a trip down the same country road led us to the preacher and our wedding day.

In the ensuing years, career took us down boulevards, thoroughfares and freeways, and the country roads of our youth were left farther and farther in the dust of our memories.

Then a trip back to the old home place about 15 years ago made us realize that it was time to finish the cycle. As we neared the Ozark Mountains, the years pealed away with the passing of each mile marker. We took the U.S. highway to the state highway to the county road to the gravel road, then stayed right at the fork. Three-quarters of a dusty mile later we discovered what we really knew all along.

Country roads never were dead ends. They led to the most important of all destinations: Home. With that simple truth in hand, we moved back to our old family farm to finish the last miles of our journey together.

Wherever country roads have taken you through the years, this special collection of stories will make the return trip pleasant to your memory. As you travel with us to work or play, to school or vacation, Janice and I know you will enjoy this journey back to the Good Old Days along the avenues called Country Roads.

Ken Tay

⊰ Contents ⊱

Those Daring Young Men • 6

Our First Automobile 8
Dad's Pride & Joy 12
My Old Tin Ford 15
The Supreme Chadwick 16
Our First Lizzie 19
Tricky Throttles 20
Dad and the Motorcar 24
Putting on the Brakes 27
Skitterbugs 29
Early Days 31

Petticoats & Puddlejumpers • 32

My Red Rocket 34
When Ma Drove the Model T 38
Some Dizzy Woman 39
I Loved That Model T 40
Black Beauty 43
The Two Sisters 44
Woman Driver 46
Life With a Ford 48
The Puddle Jumper 53
My First Car 54
How Not to Drive a Car 56

Out for a Spin • 58

Sunday Drives 60
Finding the Sun 63
Surrey With the Fringe on Top 64
Burma Shave Signs 67
Grandpa's Flivver 70
Mongolian War Wagons 74
The Speedmobile 78
A Change for the Better 82

Are We There Yet? • 84

Yellowstone for $24 86
Rambling Along in a Rumble Seat 90
Dad's "Campcar" 91
Hold Your Hat 92
My Worst Christmas Eve 94
To Grandmother's House We Go! 96
Big Bend Safari... 99
Summer Vacation 102
Old-Time Vacations.................................... 105
Cabins $1, Bedding 50 Cents Extra..................... 108
Lester's Restaurant 112
You Can't Get There From Here 116
Going to Oklahoma.................................... 120
Maine Ho! 123
Thumbing My Way 126
Westward to California 129

Against the Elements • 130

The First Mission Impossible 132
Neith Rain, Nor Snow, Nor Sleet, Nor Hail 138
Whatever Happened to Running Boards?............... 139
Covered Bridge 140
Entertaining Angels.................................... 142
Road Building 145
Oiled Roads... 147
A Winter Remembered 148
The Lantern 152
Lap Robes 154
Old Cars & Deep Snow 156
The Rumble Seat...................................... 160

Those Daring Young Men

Chapter One

Much of what I learned in my early life I learned directly or indirectly from my older brother, Dennis. Five years older than I, Dennis was first at everything. It was through him that I learned how to go to school, how to play basketball and how to handle relationships with my parents. So it was with cars and driving. Dennis was the pioneer; I took a back seat and, hopefully, learned from his experience.

Never was that more evident than the time Dennis wrecked the Pontiac. He was, if memory serves me, around 17. I don't remember the circumstances, but he had probably been to one of our Friday night town dances or some such celebration. Afterwards he left the bright lights of town behind, escorted his girlfriend home and then began the late-night curvy trek to our farm.

It could have been fatigue. It could have been a rain-slicked roadway. It could have been both. But, for whatever reason, Dennis went straight while the road went left and the old Pontiac found itself hurtling through Farmer Jones' barbwire fence and into a paddock of bewildered bovine.

Dennis assessed the situation, knowing he would be in deep trouble with Daddy if Daddy found out about the mishap. So, he extracted the Pontiac from the field, mended the fence as best he could and then, driving much more carefully now, finished his journey home. He breathed a sigh of relief as he slipped into the house and then to bed, thinking he had successfully engineered an escape from parental wrath.

At the breakfast table the next morning, he was unusually quiet. Daddy wasn't. "Where did you wreck the Pontiac?" he asked. Dennis' head snapped up from his bacon and eggs. "You did have an accident last night, didn't you?" Dennis could do nothing but confess. I don't remember the punishment; he was too old to spank, part of it probably had something to do with the loss of driving privileges until his 30th birthday or so.

After breakfast Dennis asked if I had said anything to Daddy. Heck, I didn't know anything to speak of. He was still shaking his head about it Monday morning. I wasn't confused. It was obvious to me. Mama and Daddy were clairvoyant and read Dennis' mind. Or Gabriel brought them a message from God. Or maybe they noticed the mud caked under the bumper and the barb-skinned spot on the front quarter-panel.

A few years later when it was my turn to drive, I learned from Dennis' mistake. To this day I have *never* punched through a paddock fence with a Pontiac. I guess I never was one of those daring young men in their driving machines.

—Ken Tate

Our First Automobile

By A.T. Walters

*I*f there was an opinion poll taken on the most valuable invention in the past hundred years, I would have to vote for the automobile. It is true that it piled unknown sorrow and suffering into our midst; but it has also been the greatest thing in our lives since the Garden of Eden, in my humble opinion.

When I was born before the turn of the last century, there weren't any of those machines parked around our neighborhood. I didn't see one until I was 15. That's when a neighbor went to St. Louis and came back in the cockpit of one of those bright, brass-trimmed horseless carriages. It caused more excitement than Halley's comet did in 1910!

We younger folks stood around with our hands behind us, watching and admiring this new machine. There was one thing on which we all agreed: If we ever got fully grown, got jobs and got our hands on enough money, we would be the proud owners of one of those wonders.

We scrambled out of the car and went to the farmer for help. He came to our rescue with a team of horses, and without much trouble, we were back on the road again.

My dad was a veterinarian. For many years, he had used his faithful old horse and buggy to make his house calls throughout southern Illinois.

Dad made pretty good money, but he never bothered to put it in a bank. It was 20 miles to one of those institutions, and I don't think he saw any reason to drive a horse and buggy that distance to have someone keep his money when a little secret closet in the wall could do the job just as well. Besides, Mama was around to keep an eye on it.

In the early summer of 1916, school was out and I had just received my 12th-grade certificate. I was loafing around the neighborhood, waiting for someone to offer me a job. I noticed that our parents were talking, their heads real close together, and looking rather serious. I thought there might be something cooking, but I had no idea what it might be. We kids talked it over, but we only became more confused.

A few days later we heard a roar out in front of the house and we rushed out to investigate. To our great amazement and pleasure, we found the doctor—our dad—seated under the wheel of a brand-new Maxwell touring car, fully equipped with

JAY KILLIAN

a box of tire patch, no spare tire, no air pump, and no jack. But it was new and we didn't plan on having trouble. We could buy the necessities in Cairo later and make a bank deposit on the same trip.

But first someone in our family had to learn to keep the thing between the fences to get there. I was appointed co-pilot. Dad was afraid I would scratch some paint from the fenders. I didn't learn very fast, and for some time, Dad continued using his faithful old horse and buggy.

By this time, our neighbor was having trouble with his two-year-old horseless carriage. There wasn't a garage or mechanic in the whole countryside. A plan had to be found for training a driver and a repairman for our automobile.

Mother was a faithful reader of the *Comfort Magazine*. I think it was printed in Augusta, Maine. Each month they printed instructions on how to repair an internal combustion engine, pictures and all.

We found a number of back issues and the entire family spent many hours at night smartening up on the subject. After several nights of book work, Dad said he thought it was time for graduation, and there was no better time than the present. The old *Comforts* were placed back on the shelf, then we went out for some hands-on experience.

I, as the appointed co-pilot, had not yet been under the wheel. But early one morning, Dad thought we should dig some of our cash out from between the walls and take it to a banker for safer keeping. He called the roll and loaded Mom and his six youngsters into our chariot, and started struggling over 20 miles of ruts to Cairo. After visiting our potential banker, we would buy the supplies to keep our Maxwell running.

We did very well for the first 15 miles. Then, about five miles from our destination, a farmer recognized the doctor and flagged him down to examine some of his livestock.

This is where the complications set in. It wasn't too long before Dad was back and under

the wheel. But when he stepped on the starter, no go. I got out and used the crank, and again the starter. Nothing happened.

Dad found a telephone and called a garage in Cairo for help. About an hour later, a man came out in a truck with a long chain. He hooked it onto the car and again we were traveling toward town.

On our arrival at the garage, the man said, "Five bucks, please." That was a lot of money in those days, but it was handed over.

Another man walked up. He said he was the mechanic and asked if we were having trouble. He got into the car, looked around and asked for the key. I looked at Dad and Dad looked at me, then reached deep into his pocket and handed the man the key.

He inserted it into the proper hole, gave it a twist, stepped on the starter and the motor roared. He said the trouble was easy to find. Then he smiled and said, "Five bucks, please."

We backed out of the place and drove toward the bank, hoping there would be no further decrease in our savings before we could make a deposit.

We left the bank, then bought what we needed to keep our car on the road. Just as the sun was sinking behind the distant hills, we drove into our own yard. Nobody talked much and Dad didn't get any ribbing about the key. He didn't look like he could take it.

Dad would sit around and talk about his automobile. I would look at him and smile. He wouldn't say anything.

The next Sunday evening, before church time, Dad said we would go for a short drive and get back to the meetinghouse about the right time for the preaching service. We loaded into the car, all eight of us. I looked forward and smiled.

Dad caught me at it. Frowning at me, he said, "You're so smart, I'll let *you* do the driving."

I was sure that I could do the job and moved under the wheel. With Dad as co-pilot, we moved off. I thought I was doing a pretty good

> *On our arrival at the garage, the man said, "Five bucks, please." That was a lot of money in those days, but it was handed over.*

Same 1914 model as my dad's first Maxwell, minus the top.

job—that is, until it was time to turn around and start back toward the church.

I saw a road leading up to a farmer's house. I turned in. There was a deep ditch and a narrow bridge. I missed the bridge and headed straight in, and 10 feet down.

When we came to rest at the bottom, I had my kid sister Grace astride my neck. She got a handful of my hair and said, "Albert, we will never get out of this hole."

We scrambled out of the car and went to the farmer for help. He came to our rescue with a team of horses, and without much trouble, we were back on the road again. Dad took over the piloting duties, but he didn't make it back in time to hear his favorite preacher.

Monday morning we got up bright and early and sat down to a breakfast of homegrown bacon and eggs, reinforced with a pan of hot biscuits. With breakfast behind us, I think the doctor was feeling pretty good.

He said he thought it best that we go to town for a little gas. I could do the driving.

He would go along to see that nothing drifted beyond control.

Some fellow had made the mistake of erecting a brand-new service station in a prominent downtown area. I was driving our chariot in for a refill when Dad said, "Stop." I brought her to a screaming halt. Dad said he would do the spotting at the pump.

I got out on the left side. He slid under the wheel, shifted into gear and gave her the gas. You never saw anything like it—that car leaped like a Kansas jackrabbit, headed for the pump, pillow and post, then the roof caved in on the whole works. The doctor was under there somewhere. We dug him out and found that he was still hanging together. We gave the place a good inspection, then the doctor told the man to go ahead and rebuild his station and he would pay all damages.

It took the entire crew two hours to dig our chariot out of the rubble. After taking on a small amount of gas (in a pail), we drove slowly home for a major two-week repair job. ❖

Dad's Pride & Joy

By Willard C. Loughlin

From the time Dad graduated from the Chicago Academy of Automobile Engineering and came home with a black leather suit, complete with pants, jacket and cap with a leather bill, he was the top rooster in our neighborhood. We never could figure out the purpose of the black leather suit—unless he figured he might get a chauffeur job somewhere. Certainly there were no automobiles in our neighborhood, and mighty few in the whole town of Emporia, Kan.

Dad loved cars—all of them—and his greatest joy was tearing one apart and putting it back together again. It wasn't any wonder, then, that we always had some monstrosity parked around our yard. I particularly remember a Moon and an Abbot-Detroit. He had both of them torn apart, but when he pulled in with a 1910 Velie, he didn't have much time to work on the others.

He fell in love with that Velie the minute he laid eyes on her. She had genuine black leather upholstery, shiny brass gas headlights and a big horn that let out a "*Honk!*" when the bulb was squeezed … and somebody was always ready to squeeze it. Dad didn't mind at all. He'd just grin.

Two brass rods braced the windshield. They were bolted onto the windshield and extended down to the body and did a good job of holding the windshield in place. It was a joy polishing those two rods, because nothing dressed that Velie like those two rods and the headlamps.

Dad had gone over the motor completely, and he just let the Velie sit under the pear tree until the day when he would take her on her maiden voyage. In the meantime, he decided on a shiny new paint job, and after checking out all the available colors, he decided he'd like a pretty maroon. Nobody ever saw a prettier paint job. Dad wasn't a painter of automobiles, but he put everything he had into that effort.

Finally the word went out that everything was ready. The neighbors and neighborhood kids all gathered for the show. The family was nervous, hoping that Dad had put all the parts

He fell in love with that Velie the minute he laid eyes on her. She had genuine black leather upholstery, shiny brass gas headlights and a big horn that let out a "Honk!" when the bulb was squeezed …

back again, but Dad wasn't ruffled in the least.

He crawled in and adjusted his cap with the bill turned around, and someone in the audience bravely turned the crank. Several times he cranked, and finally the motor came to life! Dad eased her out of the yard and was off in a cloud of dust down the unpaved street. There wasn't a soul coming or going so the way was clear.

The Velie really took off and Dad had to concentrate on driving. He grasped the wheel and when he had a chance, adjusted the throttle—or tried to. (The throttle was attached to the steering wheel; there were no such things as foot-feeds in those days, nor many of the other refinements that came years later.)

In the meantime, Dad whizzed by us in a cloud of dust. He was racing around the block, and at an ungodly speed, we thought. Apparently he was having trouble with something! As he tore around the block again and again, everybody held their breath and prepared to get out of the way should he lose control of the speeding car. Dad was getting excited too, for after a dozen circuits around the four-block square, he yelled at us briefly, not daring to take his hands off the wheel.

Finally, at long last, he ran out of gas, right in front of the audience. After a brief pause, he crawled out of his pride and joy and approached us with a grin. "I guess I hooked up the gas feed backwards," he said. Instead of driving it as slow as it would go, he had run it wide open during the whole race! Full speed back then wasn't what it is now, but that maroon Velie was roaring along at a terrific pace for its day.

Dad made history with that Velie. He gave all the neighbor kids rides to the swimming holes in the Cottonwood River and they loved it. We had relatives all over so we did a lot of visiting. On one night I'll never forget, our lights went out. There we were, miles from home, and there was no one to help out. Dad crawled out, walked around the car and fell into a ditch about 4 feet deep. Luckily there was no water in it.

_____

A brand new 1918 Velie Model 38 and its proud owner, Lida Tarbett Wright, sets in front of the Ritterhouse-Seitz Velie dealership in Baltimore, Md. Lida's niece, Olive Welmon Hartge and her husband, Clarence to her left, sit in the backseat; the other men in the photograph are unidentified. The photograph was found in the personal effects of Lida and Olive's niece, Jo Ann Welmon Minnig, in Mission Viego, Calif. Photograph courtesy Jo Ann Welmon Minnig and Randy Robertson.

Velie Model 58-Brougham

stood by the river. At Paddy's Mill the mill itself was gone, but nearby farm folk still used the ford there rather than driving miles farther to cross the river at a bridge.

Apparently we were on the right way to the crossing so we sailed into the water. Then we came to a dead stop, right in the middle of that gently flowing river. Water flowed right through the car. All our freshly shined shoes, our prim dresses and Sunday clothes were at the mercy of the gentle but deceiving current. Dad wasn't much for swearing, particularly since it was his judgment that had put us where we were.

He crawled out of the car to try drying the "mag." Just then, a farmer driving a hayrack pulled by two husky horses drove up and came to a stop. That farmer looked like an angel for sure. He hitched his team to the Velie and out we came!

We got to the wedding reception looking a bit worse for our experience. The Velie, shined and innocent, was ready to take us home again … this time, across a bridge. ❖

That's one time we hoped that another auto might come by and help out, but that was a lonely, quiet road. We couldn't spend the night there, so Dad decided to look for a farmhouse and borrow a lantern. Sure enough, he came trudging back with a coal-oil lantern. Its light was feeble, but by hanging it on the radiator, at least we could be seen.

We all hung out the side, straining to see the roadside so Dad could drive in the middle of the road and thus bring us home to comfortable beds and a postponed supper. It took a long time but we finally made it.

Then there was the time we dressed up in our best clothes and loaded into the Velie to attend my mother's sister's wedding some miles west of Emporia, near Saffordville, which was a lively little town in its day but is now only a faint memory. We had gotten a late start so Dad decided to take a shortcut. The ruins of two flour mills

Velie Model 58-Sport

My Old Tin Ford

—Author Unknown

Of my old tin Ford they all make fun,
They say she was born in 1901,
Well maybe she was, but this I'll bet.
She's good for many a long mile yet!

The windshield's gone and the radiator leaks,
The fan belt slips and the horsepower squeaks,
She shakes the nuts and bolts all loose—
But she gets 40 miles on a gallon of juice.

When I can't get gas I use kerosene.
I've driven her home on paraffin.
There's a rattle in the front and a grind in the rear,
And a Chinese puzzle for a steering gear.

The coils are dead and the plugs smoke fire,
The piston rings are baling wire,
But in spite of this she's pulled me through,
An' that's about all a car can do.

With high-priced cars they give you tools,
Some extra parts and a book of rules;
Wire stretchers and a pair of shears,
Are all I've carried in 15 years.

But if I live to see the day
When she falls to pieces like the "one-hoss shay,"
If old Hank Ford stays in the game,
I'll buy me another by the same old name.

"Souped up" Model T Ford made into a race car.

The Supreme Chadwick

By Dick Garretson

ll during my youth I was an avid "car buff." As soon as I was able to read, I studied pictures and descriptions of autos in advertisements. As soon as I was able to write, I wrote for catalogs. When I was 12, I was offered a dealership! I studied those catalogs, read about track races, road races, hill climbs, touring contests. I picked the incomparable Chadwick Great Six as the best of the lot.

I was fortunate to have several very wealthy relatives who often visited us during their "ganged-up" tours. Each owned several of the world's finest cars—Pierce Arrow, Winton, Locomobile, Rolls-Royce, Fiat, Bugatti, Peerless, Stevens-Duryea, Pope Toledo, Lozier, Thomas Flyer, Mathewson, Alco, Simplex. And each owned a Chadwick— their favorite—and they told me it was far superior in all ways to all their other cars! So I panted for a Chadwick!

According to the September 1952 issue of *Antique Automobile,* "Quality was Chadwick's first consideration. Their slogan was, 'Built up to a standard, not down to a price.'" How true. The Chadwick was the quietest high-powered car on the market and was practically silent in operation, and it would go faster or slower without resort to gear shift than any other car, American or European. Around 1907–1908 it was the most successful, the most powerful, the fastest, the strongest, the safest, the highest powered, the lightest, the quietest, the most easily controlled, the most dependable, the most advanced in engineering, the most luxurious.

The Chadwick was shipped, by itself, in a boxcar to my home-town of Sioux City, Iowa, where I unloaded it and drove it proudly to our farm near Howard, S.D.

The Chadwick shifted gears effortlessly. Spencer Wishart, the famous Mercer race car driver, once told me, "To change gears on a Chadwick, just breathe on the shift lever!"

The Chadwick followed the road like it was glued! Barney Oldfield, the famous Stutz and Benz race car driver, told me, after driving my Chadwick, "The front wheels follow the road and the rear wheels follow the front wheels!" This was unusual, *then*. Most cars had to be steered constantly. I owned a beautiful, ultra-modern Hudson Speedster whose front wheels stayed beautifully on track, but the rear of the car swayed back and forth from one side of the road to the other side—backseat passengers traveled more miles than the driver! One very famous, highly regarded car, the Bugatti, had to be "fought" to keep it going where the driver wanted to go! And changing its gears was absolute torture.

Came a day when I could afford a more outstanding car, and I wrote to the Chadwick factory at Pottstown, Pa.

J.T. Nichols replied that the factory had been destroyed by fire, and that one car, a Roadster with a newly designed and greatly improved Great Six motor—a much more powerful, much faster motor—had been in a distant paint shop and so escaped destruction. He priced the car. I bought it.

The car was shipped, by itself, in a boxcar to my hometown of Sioux City, Iowa, where I unloaded it and drove it proudly to our farm near Howard, S.D. Happy me!

On that first day, I stopped at Sioux Falls to eat a bite of lunch. As I stopped my car, a passerby slid his feet to an abrupt stop to stare at the long-hooded Chadwick. When he asked the make and where I was going, I answered simply "Chadwick" and "Howard." When I returned from a hasty lunch, I noticed quite a crowd of curious, admiring folks milling around my car. I was amused and have never forgotten a remark of one merchant there: "Who in Howard has enough money to buy a car like this!" That first man who had questioned me must have informed everyone there.

I had no difficulty entering my car or starting the motor. A path quickly cleared for me and I drove slowly away, with spectators waving and shouting good wishes. I lost over an hour, but it was well worth it in fond, lasting memories. What nice folks they were!

This 1907 Chadwick touring car has a huge 11.2 liter engine designed by Lee Sherman Chadwick. When first produced, Chadwick was disappointed with the performance and installed a supercharger—the first such addition to a production car in the United States. This car is one of only two Chadwicks known to exist today. The other, a fully restored race model, is also on display at the Seal Cove Auto Museum, Camden, Maine. Photo courtesy John J. Sandford.

Law officers glowered at my Chadwick like it was impossible to drive it without breaking all speed laws! It was obviously a menace to all law-abiding citizens! I once was ticketed for speeding while following a span of slow-walking mules pulling a heavily loaded dray on the main street in Parker, S.D. In Sioux City I often was stopped by police and asked how fast I was going. Usually it was 8 miles an hour.

It wasn't long before I was trying out the Chad's mighty power—138 *racehorses*—and astounding speed and effortless handling. With Mother beside me, I opened up on a twisting dirt wagon road between Vilas and Lake Madison, S.D., a distance of 28 miles. We made it in 20 minutes. There was no sand, no gravel, no paving on that road. And we had to slow down going through the outskirts of Howard and while entering Lake Madison.

Many local owners of Cads, Hups, Velies, Reos and Studebakers oft tried to keep my Chad from passing them. The result was like a snail racing a fast mail train! I could have easily passed them in second gear—and I had four speeds. When I passed them, it seemed to me that they were going full speed backwards! But there was one race I almost lost to the disgrace of my good Chadwick!

On that same stretch of road between Vilas and Lake Madison, a few miles from one of our farms, a big, red, stripped-down Fiat race car with Minnesota license plates pulled up beside me, daring me. The driver evidently was misled by my car's silent purr. He sneered disdainfully at my car and laughed at me as he ran along beside me. Little did he know that my purring car housed a mighty 760-cube motor, the largest, most powerful of any car on earth!

Of course, this driver was familiar with the Chadwick's enviable record in hill climbs, track and road races, but he evidently did not recognize my new-model car as a Chadwick. Besides, what hick in this hayseed country would know anything about racing? Nor did this driver know that the hick he was laughing at had, several times and always rather successfully, raced on tracks and in road races against the world's best drivers and the world's finest cars! And that this car he was sneering at was the very fastest production car in the whole wide world. I had 138 straining racehorses ready to turn loose on him! But fate was to take a hand in his favor.

I had a very dangerous habit of driving with my right arm draped over the right side door top (my car was right-hand drive). There was probably only one blue hornet in all of Miner County, but that one nosey buttinsky just *had* to get into my car's airstream at that one split second and get sucked up into my right shirt sleeve! It made him mad and me sorry! That vicious hornet started right in stinging at my wrist and progressively, savagely, stung me all the way up my arm and under my armpit, across my chest and down across my stomach! Then that little demon squeezed under my belt and got extra busy! *Boy—that hurt!*

The pain was excruciating and very disconcerting. I was constantly tensing, bracing, for the next painful jab, when I should have been concentrating on my driving. We were racing over bad stretches of wagon-wheel-rutted dirt road and dodging traffic at blazing speed. I had

to endure the pain or lose the race to a darned smart aleck. And shame my nice Chadwick? I endured the pain and the distraction.

My antagonist was racing alongside me. I was slowed by a car in front of me, which I recognized as the National owned by a local realtor. I was bottled in. Mr. Fiat, worried about oncoming traffic, tried to scare me into slowing and letting him crowd in ahead of me. But I had always been rather difficult to scare. I kept tailgating the car ahead. Suddenly, the driver of the National decided to join the race and sped up. This made it harder for the Fiat to pass the National, but Mr. Fiat had to either pass or drop behind me, as traffic was approaching him in the opposing lane of traffic. Races are not won by slowing up and Mr. Fiat very much wanted to win.

We started traveling over a deep, hard, rutted stretch, which, at our dizzy speed, could easily have been disastrous to all three of us—but none of us slowed. Mr. Fiat took a desperate chance. He bounced and staggered and slowed on the rough road and had difficulty keeping control of his car, but he got past the National.

As soon as the road ahead cleared of traffic, I pulled over and quickly passed both the National and the Fiat, and I led both cars by a half-mile when we entered the town of Lake Madison. I pulled up at the first service station, got out, hurriedly raced to the little boys' room, opened my clothing and brushed the stinging blue demon off my body. Sir Chadwick and I won the race, but I lost a lot of sweat and tears. The next day my right arm was swollen as large around as a she-elephant's left hind leg! And my abdomen looked like I was nine months pregnant with 9-pound octuplets! But my Chad and I had won the race. What else mattered? ❖

Our First Lizzie

By Virginia Hearn Machir

The first car my father ever owned was a 1917 Model T, purchased in 1922. It came equipped with skinny tires, isinglass curtains that snapped on in case of rain, a horn that went "Oo-*oo*-ga! Oo-*oo*-ga!" and a hand crank that was used to start the motor. My sisters and I were as proud of it as if it had been a Rolls Royce.

Father had never driven an automobile and during the first few trips, no one was permitted to talk as it distracted him from driving. If my sisters or I forgot and talked, he would roar from the front seat, "Shut up! I can't drive with all the noise!"

Once, when the car reached the slat gate that opened into our lane, instead of pushing the brake pedal, Dad just pulled back on the steering wheel and yelled, "Whoa! Whoa!" The Model T kept right on going, breaking the latch and pushing open the gate without doing any damage to the gate itself.

"Dan, did you think you were driving a team of mules?" Mom asked. But Dad soon learned the knack of navigating the Ford, even while we had conversation.

Mother learned to drive too, but she was never very good in reverse. Once she backed the Model T out of the garage, which sat at the top of the hill, and forgot to brake it. The car rolled down the hill, hit a peach tree and broke it, breaking a taillight in the process. But at least the collision stopped the car. Father never tired of telling how Mother broke the taillight and ruined the peach tree.

Our Model T gave us a jolting ride. The tires were pumped to a high pressure; it had to be 40–60 pounds of air pressure to make them hard enough to carry the car's weight. Being so hard, they did not provide a very comfortable ride.

Every tire had to have a rubber inner tube to hold the air. Father would be driving along the gravel road and we would hear a loud "Pop!"

"Another blowout!" Father would say as he pulled off the highway to fix the flat tire. He would repair the hole in the tube by gluing a small patch of rubber over it. Woe unto the motorist who forgot to carry the little kit containing the tube patches!

We didn't have bumper stickers in those days, but teenage owners of Model T's painted signs on the bodies of their cars. We saw slogans like "The Tin You Love To Touch," "Peaches, Here's Your Can," "Capacity: 5 Gals," "Come On Baby, Here's Your Rattle," "Danger: 100,000 Jolts" and "Don't Laugh, Girls, Think How You Would Look Without Paint!" We wanted Father to paint some signs on our Model T but he wouldn't hear of it.

Model T's were seen filled to capacity with teenagers, the overflow riding on the fenders. Roadsters with their tops down, containing a fellow and his date in the front seat and a pair of lovers in the back in the rumble seat, led preachers of the 1920s to expound on the evils of Mr. Ford's invention. Surely, they declared, young people were going to hell in Ford cars!

Regardless of the jokes made about the Model T, it was the most famous and popular car in automobile history. Our Model T took our family on many happy trips to Grandma's, to silent movies, county fairs and family outings. I'm glad I lived in the 1920s and 1930s and had the experience of riding in a Model T, the first automobile my father ever owned. ❖

Above: *The Love of My Life* by John Slobodnik, House of White Birches nostalgia archives

© *Neighbors* by Dave Barnhouse/Hadley Licensing 2003

Tricky Throttles

By L. Kugler

The year 1923 brought with it an innovation that would have a profound impact on the motoring public. This was the year that Henry Ford introduced the foot-operated throttle on his Model T Fords.

Foot-feed operation was not new to the automotive industry. Most all other makes and models of automobiles had this feature at their inception, but in 1923, perhaps more than 50 percent of all drivers in the United States were driving Model T Fords. Its popularity did not derive from its beauty, riding qualities or ease of handling, but it surpassed the horse and rivaled the mule as a tough and reliable mode of transportation.

When drivers made the change to the new model with a foot feed or to another brand of automobile that had one, the transition was confusing at best, and sometimes downright terrifying when things got out of hand.

Imagine, if you can, the antics of an automobile when the operator, oriented to hand-throttle operation—and now needing to suddenly slow or stop his car—inadvertently placed his foot on the wrong pedal. Accustomed to having only the brake pedal in that approximate location on the floor, the immediate reflex was to stomp down hard when the car suddenly surged forward or backward. But the harder he pushed, the faster he went and the faster he went, the harder he pushed.

The only thing that could stop a machine, once the driver panicked, was an immovable object.

Dad bought our first car, a 1913 Model T, in 1918 and he got along with it very well. Then, in 1922, he traded it in on a brand-new Model T. It was his pride and joy; he cared for it with loving hands; it was never abused. He didn't bring it home until he had built a new car shed to keep it in. (In those days, you only put your car in a "garage" if it needed repairs; at home you kept it in a "car shed.") Eight straight years that little Ford never sat out in the weather overnight.

For 12 years Dad had been driving with a hand-operated gas feed, and then, in 1930, with a little urging on our part, he decided to buy a "shift car," as we called cars with stick-shift transmissions.

I took Dad to town one beautiful spring day to see if we could find a car that would fit both his fancy and his purse. We went to see Roscoe Moran, an auto salesman who had once been a neighbor boy. Even in those days, used auto salesmen had glib tongues, but Dad felt he could trust Roscoe.

And he had just what we were looking for—a small, 1925 Chevrolet coupe. It had front-opening doors and jet black paint that was kept shiny by a daily wipe-down with a kerosene-soaked rag.

Roscoe told us, as expected, that it had belonged to the little old lady who lived across the street; he quickly added that at present, she was in Florida, caring for a sick sister. The odometer had only 500 miles on it, but as we found later, it wasn't working.

A touch of Roscoe's toe to the starter button brought the four-cylinder motor to instant life. The Chevrolet was famous for its starting qualities in those days of hard-starting cars, and the little Chevy sat there purring quietly, a far cry from the backfiring habits of the Model T. Dad's eyes sparkled and he fell hard—or maybe it was just infatuation. No more getting slapped around by that back-kicking crank on the Model T; he would have a self-starting car now.

"The old lady," Roscoe said, "sold the car because she was afraid of its tremendously fast acceleration. It will climb a mountain off the road in low or reverse gear," he claimed. That proved to be true. Dad bought the car for $200. A neighbor who had hitchhiked a ride to town drove the car home for us. That night, the 1922 Model T had to sit outside, the little coupe taking its place in the car shed.

The next day, Dad had to learn to drive all over again. A nearby stubble field, not yet plowed for corn planting, was the training ground.

Getting the foot-feed power application in sync with the clutch release seemed to be his biggest problem. After a few jerky starts and stops and a couple of trips around the 2-acre field, I left him to spend the day practicing while I took his place behind the plow in another field.

That evening when I came in, the 2-acre plot looked like the dirt race track at the county fairgrounds. Our training course, we came to realize later, was faulty in one respect. Running at 5–10 miles per hour in very loose dirt on a flat area had given Dad no need to switch his foot from foot feed to brake pedal from time to time, and that was a phase of the training that he really needed.

Figuring that he had mastered all there was to know about driving a shift car, and scoffing at the big

to-do made about the training process, he left the car sitting at the edge of the field. We drove it into the shed for him later.

After the chores were done and supper eaten, we noticed that the car-shed doors were again open. We peeked in and then tiptoed away. Dad was wiping the dust and grime from his newfound love with an old woolen sock soaked in kerosene.

Next morning at breakfast, I offered very gently to move the Chevy to the field for another get-acquainted session. But he answered as I'd expected: "Heck, no." I humbly kept my tongue to myself and my eyes on my plate. We finished eating in silence; even Mom was quiet, and that was a switch from the norm. A couple of worry wrinkles had appeared over her eyes.

Dad finished his breakfast, slapped his old straw hat on his head and announced, "After I get the calves fed, I'm going to drive to the store to get some gas. If you don't think I can drive that Chevy, come along."

I heard Mom's sigh of relief at the offer. It was against my better judgement, but with Mom's anxious eyes on me, I replied, "OK, I'd like to go along." That was a big fib, but I never had to prove its sincerity.

When Dad went to the shed to get his car out, I found reason to be behind the woodpile, peeking out only when I heard the motor start. A premonition of impending disaster weighing heavily on me, I fully expected to see that little car blast through the rear of the building in a mass of splintered two-by-fours and siding. Not so! A little grating of the gears and then she was coming out of there, carburetor full and open in reverse. The nonskid design of the rear tires performed well, and it jumped into full-speed reverse almost at once. Dad, pushing hard forward on the steering wheel, was howling, "Whoa, you beast! Whoa! Whoaaaaaa!"

Figuring that he had mastered all there was to know about driving a "shift car," and scoffing at the big to-do made about the training process, he left the car sitting at the edge of the field. We drove it into the shed for him later.

The motor moaned in anguish at the driver's unreasonable demands. It is hard to say just what would have transpired had it not been for the big elm tree 100 feet from the shed. The car hit the tree dead center and the spring steel bumper, designed to withstand any impact, recoiled and tossed the car 30 feet forward, airborne. The motor screamed in protest and then the tires were digging in again, the car hurtling backward to give the elm another try. Four times it tried, each butt becoming a little less violent, until, conceding defeat, the motor finally died. The big elm, standing stately and arrogant, never shed a leaf.

As I came running up, the car, its rear tires and motor smoking from its all-out effort, was rocking violently as Dad tried in vain to find the correct knob to pull to open the front door.

A mixture of German and lumber-camp jargon new to me was being directed at the little car. When I turned the outside door handle, it exploded outward to send me sprawling. As Dad hit the ground, he aimed a kick at my posterior, calculated to wipe the big grin off my face. It missed. Then he grabbed the door in both hands, slamming it so hard that the window glass shattered into tiny pieces.

I backed off. It just was not the time to discuss Dad's driving talents.

He gingerly rubbed the growing knot on the back of his head and checked his head for blood. Retrieving his hat through the broken window, he set it well forward on his head and started for the barn. Halfway there, he turned and bellowed, "Get that ---- thing out of here! Take it back to Roscoe!" I was on my way within the hour.

Never again did the 1922 Model T have to relinquish its place of honor in its own little sheltering shed. ❖

Dad and the Motorcar

By Floyd E. Hutcheson

My dad never seemed to reconcile himself to the motorcar. To him, the gasoline-powered contraption was a demon. It was the summer of 1919 before Dad could bring himself to keep up with the times and purchase an automobile. His first was a Model T touring car with cloth top, demountable side curtains and isinglass windows. The car was shiny black. Henry Ford had said that customers could have a choice of colors—so long as the color was black.

Dad bought the automobile from the dealer in our hometown. Dad must have been a challenging customer; he had a well-known reputation as a shrewd horseman and trader. No doubt his horse-trading instincts went to work, because he wound up trading a matched pair of mules on the transaction.

The dealer gave Dad a very brief lesson on how to operate his new possession, and so, along about 5 o'clock on a Saturday afternoon, our shiny automobile sat near the yard gate at the end of our long "in-drive."

After Sunday dinner the next day, Dad invited the entire family to go for a ride in the new car. My two sisters, two brothers and I wedged ourselves in the backseat. Mother sat stiffly in the front seat while Dad cranked the motor to get it started. He entered the driving compartment by throwing one leg over the driver's side, which had no door, and settling himself on the cushions behind the steering wheel.

The steering column on the Model T held two hand levers, one on the left and one on the right. The lever on the left was the "spark," which had to be retarded before cranking the motor by hand since an advanced spark caused the motor to "kick." Many a motorist suffered a broken arm or a badly sprained wrist because he had forgotten to retard the spark. The right-hand lever was a control for regulating the amount of gas to the engine and thus controlling the speed of the vehicle. The driver usually moved the lever with one or two fingers of his right hand while still grasping the steering wheel.

The family was all in place for a thrilling, Sunday-afternoon motor trip. Dad got the auto to moving. It was his intention to make a right-hand U-turn and thus proceed down our lane to the county road. But as he turned the steering wheel, his finger inadvertently advanced the gas lever. The mechanical monster leaped into acceleration, and Dad could not finish his U-turn. We roared out across the alfalfa field, barely missing farm machinery and dodging hummocks of hay.

Dad was determined, so we bounced over a shallow ditch onto the county road some 80 rods from our farm entrance. Not a sound came from the backseat (we didn't dare). Mother, who was prepared for the "white-knuckle" drive anyway, murmured her favorite saying, "For mercy sake." I never knew whether the words were intended as an expletive or a short prayer.

A ride around the square mile and back ended our first—and for some of us, our *last*—Sunday-afternoon pleasure trip with Dad at the wheel.

The next several weeks were uneventful as far as Dad and his motorcar were concerned. Then came the Saturday evening when the family returned from town, having spent the evening shopping and buying groceries for the following week.

We had no garage, so the car was stored in the driveway of our two-story barn, which was built into the hillside. This driveway was really

A group of Fords and their drivers downtown.

the second story, or the hay and grain loft. It was entered on the hill side of the barn by a short, steep ramp. At the far end of the driveway was a sturdy workbench. There was no door at the other end of the driveway, which was about 15 feet above the ground. The horses were tied in stalls below, on the first level.

On that fateful evening, Dad breezed easily into the farmyard and attempted to drive up the ramp without stopping, but he didn't make it on the first try. He backed the car down the ramp and ordered all passengers out. "Also, unload the groceries." After everyone was out, Dad took a wide-open-throttle run at the ramp. He made it easily, but then he forgot how to stop.

We were carrying boxes of groceries to the house when we heard a loud crash from the barn, followed by the tinkle of falling glass. All was pitch-dark. Shortly after the crash, there was a scream of horses and a terrible commotion in the horse barn.

Dad's Model T had collided with the heavy workbench, the corner of which rammed

through the radiator and smashed the engine block. The hot water from the radiator streamed through the floor cracks and onto the horses below. The horses broke loose and charged through the barn's half-door, stampeding into the night. Dad voiced a few choice expletives, which, unlike Mother's, were unmistakably not prayerlike.

The disaster ended our motoring for many months. For an entire year, the car sat on blocks in the barn while the family returned to using the spring wagon and the driving team as our only means of transportation.

That winter, we all quickly learned that the motorcar and "The Saturday-Night Crash" were not fit subjects for jest or even quiet conversation.

Time and the pressure of progress mellowed Dad somewhat. Eventually our crippled pride and joy was towed away ignominiously behind a truck, and three days later, we had our second automobile. But Dad never trusted a "mechanical monster" again. ❖

Brakes to trust ...quick and quiet!

The 1946 Ford offers more advances than most pre-war yearly models! There's new-styled smartness throughout. Still more over-all economy . . . Here is a big car—with increased power —and new *oversize* hydraulic brakes for quick and quiet stops . . . (And what a ride! *So level. So smooth and gentle*—thanks to new slow-action springs) . . . Inside you'll find new richness. Colorful fabrics—soft to the touch—and smartly tailored to the broad, deep seats . . . There's a choice of engines—both with new thrift features to save gas and oil. The V-8, now stepped-up from 90 to 100 horsepower—the 90 horsepower Six . . . All in all, they're the smartest, finest Ford cars ever built. See for yourself. Your Ford dealer will be happy to show them to you.   *FORD MOTOR COMPANY*

There's a *Ford* in your future!

TUNE IN . . . THE FORD SHOW . . . CBS, Tuesdays. 10-10:30 P.M. E.S.T.   THE FORD SUNDAY EVENING HOUR . . . ABC, Sundays. 8-9 P.M., E.S.T.

1946 Ford ad, House of White Birches nostalgia archives

Putting On the Brakes

By Mary Griffin-Strother

Once upon a year, Grandpa Will bought a new Model T Ford. He personally never learned to drive, so each year, one of his sons was given the task of driving Grandpa back to his old home place for his annual pilgrimage. This was a duty all four brothers worked diligently to avoid, for Grandpa Will firmly believed in getting there and getting back. The highest number on the speedometer was the lowest he would settle for.

One year my father was the designated driver. He and two of his sisters climbed aboard, with Grandpa Will riding shotgun. During the 190-mile drive, my grandfather regularly broke the strained silence: "Faster, Jack. Won't this thing go faster?" But my father continued at the regular pace, ignoring Grandpa Will's griping and grumbling.

Then would come the long, boring hours of waiting while Grandpa visited with family and friends. My father and his sisters were relieved when Grandpa Will finally ordered, "Load 'er up and head 'er out, Jack. Let's head for flatland country and home cooking."

The roads through the hills were little more than wagon tracks, with trees growing so close to the trail that it was an effort to keep the Model T between them. At the top of one particularly steep hill, Grandpa yelled above the *chug chug* of the engine, "Pull 'er ears back, Jack, and let 'er rip!" My father squeezed together the two levers that regulated the gas flow, and down the hill they flew.

Suddenly Grandpa Will became alarmed at the speed with which they were approaching the bottom of the hill. Bracing himself and hanging on to the car door, he yelled, "Whooooooooaaa, Jack!"

When the car showed no sign of slowing, Grandpa Will yelled, "I'll stop this thing myself!" He proceeded to stick his arm out the window and latch onto a sturdy young sapling beside the road.

Other than breaking his arm in three places and nearly pulling himself out of the speeding vehicle, Grandpa accomplished exactly nothing. They made it to the bottom of the hill, sought medical attention for Grandpa Will in the next town, and finally made it home sometime into the night.

On Grandpa's next pilgrimage back to the old home place, the son whose misfortune it was to drive had a much easier job. Grandpa Will made the trip in silence, letting his son set the pace while he enjoyed the scenery. ❖

The roads were terrible, and posted badly or not at all; you had to equip yourself against a hundred mishaps, ninety-three of which actually happened—but you were often up to your hubcaps in pleasure.

A Better Value For The 1923 Buick Open Cars

Buick open cars bring a comfort and convenience to winter driving, surpassed only by the more expensive closed models.

Close fitting curtains, that open with the doors, are provided with a weather strip of special design to seal their joints. The tight fitting windshield is adjustable from the inside, and with the curtains, insures a snug and cozy interior.

A more satisfying sense of safety is found in the wide visibility that the curtain design affords and in the signal pocket for the driver.

Combining this weather protection with the traditional Buick performance completes a value in a car that has no superior.

The Buick Line for 1923 Comprises Fourteen Models:

Fours—2 Pass. Roadster, $865; 5 Pass. Touring, $885; 3 Pass. Coupe, $1175; 5 Pass. Sedan, $1395; 5 Pass. Touring Sedan, $1325. Sixes—2 Pass. Roadster, $1175; 5 Pass. Touring, $1195; 5 Pass. Touring Sedan, $1935; 5 Pass. Sedan, $1985; 4 Pass. Coupe, $1895; 7 Pass. Touring, $1435; 7 Pass. Sedan, $2195; Sport Roadster, $1625; Sport Touring, $1675. Prices f. o. b. Buick Factories; government tax to be added.

WHEN BETTER AUTOMOBILES ARE BUILT. BUICK WILL BUILD THEM

BUICK MOTOR COMPANY, FLINT, MICHIGAN
Division of General Motors Corporation

Pioneer Builders of Valve-in-Head Motor Cars
Branches in All Principal Cities—Dealers Everywhere

[1923]

Skitterbugs

By J.P. Holden

A few years back I heard a commercial for Chevrolet. The text went something like this: "It's not just your car, it's your freedom!" It reminded me of Grandpa. He didn't own a Chevy, but I know his first automobile, a Buick, was not just a car. It was, in fact, his freedom.

I'm afraid it took the automobile to feed Grandpa's passion for speed. You see, it wasn't just freedom Gramps craved; it was the knowledge that suddenly he could move at a pace that would cause the widow ladies in the county to sit up and take notice. Grandma had been gone for several years and Gramps was lonesome. There was no one to tell him to slow down. There was no one to scold him for taking a hairpin turn or for leaning on the horn—womanly things, the things that Grandma would've picked up on.

Of course an automobile hadn't always figured in Gramps' plans. He certainly wasn't the first to run out and buy one. For one thing, Gramps loved Flame, his faithful old dobbin. Flame was a strong, steady and dependable means of transport. More than that, Flame was a friend. Somehow Gramps couldn't see putting his best horse out to pasture—swapping four fine legs for a skitterbug on wheels. Even if Jake Crowley had done that very thing.

Jake Crowley! How Gramps despised that man! "The town sport," everyone called him. Moneyed, cocky, good-looking and always first to try something new. Jake's "something new" was a snazzy Marmon, a car with speed, looks and quality—a car that made Gramps and his horse look pretty outdated.

"When you gonna catch up to the times?" Jake asked one Saturday when he and Gramps met.

Gramps watched, squinty-eyed, as Jake ran his handkerchief over the car's gleaming green body. "This baby can outrun a train."

"Can't see why anyone would want one of them infernal contraptions anyway!" Gramps declared. "All that noise. Like to scare a person clean out of his wits. There ought to be a law against 'em. Yes indeed, there ought to be a law." Gramps would have liked nothing more than to see the return of horses to the streets. But deep down, I think he knew that the automobile was progress. And you couldn't stop progress.

As more and more of Gramps' neighbors bought cars, Gramps had less and less to say against the "skitterbugs." His conversion to the automobile was hastened when his best friend, Willard Hollander, took delivery on a Model T. Willard lived down the road just a little. Gramps didn't even bother to saddle Flame. Perhaps he couldn't bear to. But he wasted no time getting over to see Willard's new mode of transportation.

Willard and Gramps walked over to where the black monster stood. Shiny, sleek and immaculate, the beast seemed to issue a challenge. An open job, the T had wooden-spoked wheels, mudguards and a "man-sized" steering wheel. It looked just a little intimidating. But this time Gramps was really and truly fascinated.

"How fast'll it go?" he asked.

Willard took out his Prince Albert tobacco and gave the can a thump with his thumb and middle finger. He was a tall, lean, ramrod-straight man with brown hair and piercing blue eyes. The eyes were beaming at Gramps when he boasted, "Fast enough to cause Ida St. Clair to blush."

Ida St. Clair was just about the most eligible widow woman in the area. Though she wasn't committed to any of the bachelors Gramps knew of, she did spend a lot of time in the company of Jake Crowley.

That did it for Gramps! It wasn't going to be the easiest thing in the world to put old Flame out to pasture.

But allowing the likes of Jake Crowley to make time with Ida was simply unthinkable!

A day or so later, a man drove a big, long-hooded Buick into Gramps' yard. The man was dressed in plaid. He had the look and the patter of a salesman.

"Wanta take her for a drive?"

Gramps couldn't resist any longer. There was a boyish gleam in his eyes as he watched the salesman point out every feature on the car.

"And that there is the way to stop her, now, isn't it?" Gramps asked.

"That's correct," replied the salesman, climbing in beside Gramps. "It's really very simple. You'll see."

In his eagerness, Gramps started the car at full throttle and the Buick bolted down the road in a cloud of dust. Even the salesman was beginning to panic; he hadn't realized that Gramps was out to set a record. He didn't know a thing, you see, about Jake Crowley and Ida St Clair.

Then something went wrong. I suppose Gramps finally began to realize that he wasn't totally in control of his newfangled beast. At any rate he nearly froze on the steering wheel. The Buick tore through Willard Hollander's yard and headed for a direct hit on his best friend's pigeon loft.

"Whoa, blast you, whoa!" Gramps pulled back hard on the wheel, but there was no response.

Grabbing the wheel, the salesman veered the car away from the loft and yanked the emergency brake. "My dear man," he bellowed, "this is not a horse!"

Well, it was quite some time before Gramps would even talk about cars after that. He'd come close to destroying his friendship with Willard, not to mention killing himself and the automobile salesman.

The gossip traveled. Gramps heard that Jake Crowley and Ida St Clair were going to tie the knot. They'd be taking their honeymoon trip in that big, snazzy green Marmon. Probably honk the blasted horn every time they passed his place. How that would grate!

The next day Gramps asked Willard if he'd teach him to drive. Willard, being the forgiving friend, agreed. They climbed into the T and Willard made a careful point of demonstrating

Enjoying a Sunday Drive by Tole, House of White Birches nostalgia archives

the car's brake. "It doesn't respond to verbal commands, ya know," he added trying to keep from grinning.

Willard drove for a while, then switched places with Gramps. "It's your turn now. Just remember to keep your head on."

Gramps nodded, clutching the wheel till his knuckles turned white. Everything would be fine. "You're doin' just fine," bragged Willard as the car approached Garden Valley Road.

Then it happened. Jake Crowley pulled ahead of the T. His hand hit the horn, and the sound was something like the honk of a Canada goose—only louder, *much* louder.

"Goll-darn speedbug! We'll show him, Willard. Hang on!" Gramps gunned the thing for all it was worth and shot down the hill like a bullet. "We're going to give that jackrabbit a run fer his money!"

"Slow down, Martin!" yelled Willard. "We can't run competition with Crowley's car. You'll only get us both killed trying!"

"Is this as fast as she's able to go, Will?" asked Gramps with irritation.

Willard didn't answer. He yanked the wheel from Gramps and promptly pulled into a ditch.

"I'm driving from here on in, Martin. Both me and my car would like to add a few more miles before going to the junkyard."

"Don't know what in blazes come over me, Will," Gramps said. "I guess I'm just not ready for the automobile."

That evening Gramps went out to the barn. He laid a big gnarled hand aside old Flame's head and gave her a gentle pat. "Guess you and I'll stick together from now on, girl. You may not be able to outrun them autos, but you're a whole lot safer."

Then, with a pop and a clatter, Jake Crowley sped by in his big green Marmon. He honked and waved as if nothing had ever happened between him and Gramps.

"Blasted skitterbugs, anyway!" said Gramps. Then to Jake he yelled, "Get a horse!" ❖

Early Days

By G.S. Corpe

Early in 1914, my brother and I opened a little Ford automobile agency in El Monte, Calif. El Monte then was a small town about 12 miles east of Los Angeles. The Ford Motor Company had a branch on Olive Street in Los Angeles and sold cars for cash only, directly to buyers, with no other dealers in the city.

We got our cars from Detroit by railroad freight. Six, seven or eight cars were shipped in a boxcar, knocked down. We would unload them at the depot, put the wheels on and tow them to our garage, where the running boards, fenders, lamps, etc. were installed and the cars readied for sale.

Selling automobiles in those days was a pioneering experience! Most of our buyers had never driven a car before, so they had to be taught how to drive a car. Most knew how to drive horses, but for some reason I still can't figure out, when they got hold of the steering wheel on a Model T Ford, they would steer the car to the left when they intended to go right and vice versa! Some hair-raising experiences resulted! Teaching buyers to drive was a large part of our selling expense in those days.

Trade-ins of used cars were almost unknown until after the First World War, around 1919–1920.

The cars all came with smooth-tread tires, so they couldn't get good traction on wet roads or in mud. We sold chains to be put on when it rained. There was no snow, of course, in Southern California, but drivers always put on chains in wet weather.

Our little garage, which was in the rear of a blacksmith shop, really saw an increase in business after the end of World War I. We sold about 750 Model T cars and about 450 Fordson tractors each year, and we had several dozen employees. The automobile business had arrived! ❖

© *Just One More* by John Sloane

Petticoats & Puddlejumpers

Chapter Two

There was a time when petticoats and puddlejumpers just didn't go together. Maybe what I should say is there was a time when a petticoat was not a common sight in the driver's seat of a puddlejumper.

My Grandma Tate never drove, and neither did Grandma Stamps, my mother's mother. Mama herself only drove when absolute necessity forced her. When Janice married me at the tender age of 18, neither she nor her mother drove. In fact, she didn't express a lot of interest in driving, but after four years of marriage, I insisted that her petticoats find their way to the driver's seat of our old Ford.

So, I became a driving instructor. After several weeks of coughing starts and burning clutches along the gravel road we lived on, she finally had the courage to take to the pavement. It was six months or more before she braved "city" driving. The nearest town of any size was about 25 miles away and had the "huge" population of over 6,000 people.

To be honest, that made *me* more of a nervous wreck than her. In town there were more obstacles for her to maneuver around than out on the farm. Turns at intersections probably caused more consternation than any other part of the traumatic experience. If she turned too sharply, the back wheel would mount the curb and jolt us unceremoniously when we found the road again. Compensating for that, she turned too widely and nearly into oncoming cars.

If I have high blood pressure today, it was probably rooted in those white-knuckled driving lessons.

Then a marvelous thing happened. Janice went from being scared to venture out onto the highway to actually enjoying it! No more waiting for me to take her shopping, as her mother and grandmothers before her had. She had the freedom to go where and when she wanted.

I remember the first time she chauffeured me, not in a driving lesson, but just because it was a beautiful spring day and she wanted me to go along for the ride. She bought some flowers to set out in her flower bed, and a potted violet to put in the kitchen window—but I think it was just an excuse to let me know I could give my white knuckles a rest.

Now, decades later, she has safely seen countless miles in all of the successive Tin Lizzies we've owned since those early days. The years of driving children to ball games, 4-H meetings and piano lessons behind her, she and I now enjoy more leisurely trips to antique stores, flea markets and, yes, the occasional flower stand where she still can't pass up a potted violet.

Yes, I still let her drive most of the time. It's my way to pay tribute to those petticoats and puddlejumpers back in the Good Old Days.

—Ken Tate

My Red Rocket

By Gloria Edmondson

Our oldest son, Wiley, once bought a car for a dollar. He had just started his second year of college and was working as a stock boy for a supermarket after class. You would think he could have afforded to spend at least $10!

"Wait till you see it, Ma, it's really something!" It was indeed.

The boys and their father had to drag it, kicking and screaming, into the driveway. It had been rusting for years in back of a garage. The owners, finally despairing of the clutter, found a willing victim to haul it off, thus saving the cost of a tow to a junkyard, to say nothing of the costly problems that go with aging derelicts. And there was no other way to describe the ancient Willys station wagon.

The white paint that disguised its original color was peeling off in large, curling flakes. One back window was starred with multiple cracks. Inside, the seats oozed dingy stuffing. Two tires were flat. The rusting motor was a mechanic's nightmare, and whatever covered the ceiling was hanging in ghostly shreds like Spanish moss. I could only reason that my husband had taken leave of his senses to allow this automotive abomination into our driveway.

"Nice going, gang," I commented. "You should have charged the man for hauling it off."

Chauvinists that they are, they just smiled at me patronizingly. They always did that if I said anything about their wheeling and dealing in cars. My husband and son, Brian, looked like they'd just inherited the Hope diamond. Wiley, who lacked their mechanical expertise, seemed pleased that he'd provided them with a new toy.

One good thing happened as a result: They were finally clearing out the garage. The ancient

My car? MY CAR! The goofy monstrosity was suddenly undergoing a "Mr. Hyde to Dr. Jekyll" switch. The old girl and I hit it off beautifully. We went everywhere together.

wreck was lovingly shoved inside for plastic surgery, heart transplant, etc. My only consolation was that with the overhead door shut, nobody would know that we had it.

Their first order of business was to remove the ugly, flaking paint. An interested neighbor joined the group in the garage. They were all soon slopping away with solvent on one side, and burning with an acetylene torch on the other.

Our daughter, Dale, intruded into their "man's world" for a peek, then stayed to put out the fire when one of the fenders began to burn from the efforts of the pyromaniacs with the torch. During the resulting pandemonium, while the men and boys ran around screaming for a bucket of water, Dale whipped off her old jacket and smothered the flames in a split second. The sheepish males went silently back to work.

The last of the paint was finally peeled from the old hulk, revealing the body to be in good, solid shape. The fenders were a quarter of an inch thick! They produced a satisfying "bong" when thumped. The garage crew beamed. "They sure don't make 'em like that anymore!"

A chain hoist was rigged over a heavy beam for removing the vital organ. The Dr. Frankensteins hunched over the front of the car for hours, disconnecting all the arteries before the vehicle's stubborn, rusty heart could be removed to the workbench. Fifteen-year-old Brian and his dad were at the height of their glory.

Warshawski's in Chicago and the local junkyards supplied replacement parts. I was sometimes recruited to visit the auto wrecker's place with a list. It was uncanny how they could pinpoint a vehicle exactly the same as the one undergoing surgery in our garage: "Yes, ma'am, it's in the second row, fourth stack, third from the bottom." It would take a while to get at the sandwiched parts, but we didn't have any options.

Meanwhile, back in the "operating room," the body was water-sanded, then spray-painted with rustproofing red primer.

Brian poked his head into the kitchen while I was peeling potatoes. "What color would you like, Mom?"

"I get to pick? Oh, paint it red," I replied. "It's so funny looking, there's no point in trying to hide it," I replied.

"I'll tell Dad. He says that's going to be your car since you don't have one."

I sucked on the finger I'd just peeled and shoved the potatoes aside. *My* car? MY CAR! The goofy monstrosity was suddenly undergoing a "Mr. Hyde to Dr. Jekyll" switch. Yes. It was actually an interesting, durable antique. (Never look a gift car in the grill!) I wouldn't have to pry car keys out of begrudging fingers any more. My own car! I'd be free as a bird! (At least when it wasn't wash day, cleaning time, or interfering with meals.) I let the heady sensation envelop me as I tripped out to the garage to see how they were doing with "my baby."

It wasn't nearly as grotesque as I'd thought at first. In fact, there was an air of pristine dignity about it, now that it was all cleaned up. Being 3 feet taller than anything on the road (not counting the 18-wheelers) made for an excellent view out all the windows.

The seats had been upholstered; the motor repaired and returned to its nest under the hood; the broken window replaced; and the bright red paint sparkled like red Jell-O. The addition of two good tires put the car back on the road. When the engine was started, all four cylinders percolated like happy coffeepots! The two mechanics, father and son, grinned from ear to ear as they thumped each other on the back. Wilbur and Orville couldn't have been any prouder.

The old girl and I hit it off beautifully. We went everywhere together. Occasionally a part gave out; then it was back to the junkyards.

Speed was definitely not one of the reconstituted invalid's strong points. At 40 mph, strange vibrations would wrack the ancient framework.

I usually scooted along at a pace suitable to both our bodies. Disconnected kidneys I did not need!

One warm spring day, I had a phone call from Dale: "Mom, could you come and bring some water and a radiator hose for my Buick? I'm stranded over here on Butterfield Road near Highway 53. The hose split and all the water boiled out."

None of the service stations had the right size hose. A mechanic suggested that we might make it home by wrapping up the split. I grabbed the adhesive tape out of the medicine cabinet, filled a gallon jug with water and chugged off to the rescue.

There she was, pacing by the side of the road. She filled the radiator while I taped the split hose.

"The man at the station said we should be able to get home with it if you go easy," I said. "I'll follow you. Take the first side road that goes into town."

We pulled out together, the Buick in the lead. Then, she was *off*—just like they'd shot the starting gun at the Indianapolis 500! I couldn't believe it!

My red dinosaur and I putzed along in the dust as the big Buick got smaller and smaller. I pushed the gas pedal to the floor and held it there. Slowly the needle climbed to 35 … then 40 … 45. … The old girl was shaking with palsy. We hit 50 and I just *knew* the wheels where only touching every 10 feet!

Dale was moving out again. I could now clearly see a spume of white vapor trailing behind her; she was zipping along so fast that she didn't notice it. We inched up behind her and I leaned on the horn, but she only pulled away from us. My bumper was rattling with the exertion. Her radiator wasn't the only thing that was steaming—*I* was too!

For the next mile and a half, we hung on her vapor trail like it was the last lifeboat off the Titanic! I beeped the horn repeatedly but to no avail. Finally she slowed and headed for the curb on the side road we'd turned onto. I sat shaking behind the wheel of my red rocket. She tripped over to say, "It just up and quit on me, Mom."

When I regained my voice I sputtered, "Didn't you hear my horn, you birdbrain? I *told* you to take it easy! You probably blew the engine!"

"I only went a little over 50. Was that your horn? I thought it was one of those big semi trucks trying to pass both of us! Your car sticks up so far I couldn't tell what was in back of you."

"Well," I responded, "you're in town now. It's only a mile hike to the nearest station." I drove off in disgust, leaving her gaping by the side of the road.

The Perils of Pauline had nothing on me with that car! One day the brakes went out as I was going into town. I tried banking it against the higher curbs, but went up and over. The steepest part of the hilly street was ahead of me. I put the car in low, said a prayer, and hoped we could stop after we turned into the gas station at the bottom. We made the turn at a pretty good clip, but the incline into the station helped slow us. We shuddered to a halt 6 inches from the huge garage door.

Another time, as I crawled home in it from my part-time job, an ice storm hit. The heater and defrost became so frightened that they gave up the ghost together. I scraped frantically at the shield of ice on the inside and outside of my windows as the inside rapidly became a deep

1948 Willys-Overland Motors ad, House of White Birches nostalgia archives

freeze. On slippery streets, the car went downhill sideways, even at 5 miles per hour.

The recounting of these horror stories gave my husband fits. He finally announced that he was selling the car to a friend for $150—"to keep you from getting killed in it," he said. The friend made his own improvements, then sold it to a man who owned a service station for $350.

The latest owner is reported to have sunk a fortune in the old car. He added new bucket seats, a tape deck and stereo speaker system, upholstered the entire interior, and changed the transmission and motor. He covered the fire-engine red with an incredibly expensive custom paint job.

"You just would not believe what this guy did to your old Willys," our friend chuckled. "You know, it's just like putting lace on a bowling ball." ❖

When Ma Drove the Model T

By Caroline Black

It was a hot, sunny day in the fall of 1928. The threshers were busily working at the small farm below ours and were looking forward to the supper they would share that evening.

Ma had reason to be concerned. Soon they would come to our farm to thresh oats and Pa had not bought the ground beef she needed to make a meat loaf for the farmers' supper.

Ma never swore, but with eight children to feed and no time on her hands, she was upset. Without saying a word, she grabbed her pocketbook and went out the door.

We had an old Model T and Pa was the only one who drove it. Ma had never driven before, but Ma was a smart woman, and very observant. When she went toward the car, I said, "Ma, you aren't going to drive!" But her jaw was set as she opened the door to the car and climbed in. I prayed, "Oh God, watch over her."

The car started up and rumbled down our dirt road past the farm where the threshing was in progress. The men were unloading a flat hay wagon. I could see Pa take his pipe from his mouth as they watched Ma drive past.

I never left the window until I saw the Model T coming up the road and through our yard past the trees, stopping where it had started. I asked, "Did you get the meat?"

"You bet I did," Ma replied.

She lived to be 84 and never drove again. ❖

Some Dizzy Woman

By Alice Connor Kennedy

Aunt Kathryn got her driver's license in 1932 and for the next 50 years was the world's worst driver. She never had an accident, but I'm sure she unwittingly caused a few. Her top speed was 35 miles per hour and anyone doing 45 was "a speed demon."

One morning, feeling especially brave, Aunt Kathryn decided to drive from her home in Old Saybrook to our house in Fair Haven 30 miles away. Route 1 was the only highway available at that time. It was a two-lane, twisty road with few places to pass. Kathryn drove sedately with her hand brake on, causing car and truck drivers to honk and make furious arm gestures. It took her at least an hour to make the journey and she arrived exhausted.

After a pleasant visit with my mother, Kathryn began her journey home. As she reached the corner of our street she noticed a long line of cars moving slowly along … now *these* were her kind of people. So she slipped in behind a large open car. Then she realized there were people standing all along the sidewalks, waving and cheering. Being a friendly soul, Aunt Kathryn waved and smiled back.

Suddenly, a fierce-looking man appeared at the door of her car. He banged on the window and yelled something. Since Aunt Kathryn always drove with the windows shut and doors locked, she thought he was some kind of lunatic and ignored him. Then another man began banging on the opposite door and he was joined by a state trooper. Aunt Kathryn was terrified by now, but since her husband was a trooper, she felt she had to respond.

Rolling down the window a few inches, she said, "Yes, officer? What seems to be the matter?"

The trooper looked at her in astonishment. "My goodness, lady, don't you know where you are? Don't you know who's in the car in front of you?"

Aunt Kathryn took a closer look at the large, open touring car ahead of her. There, in all his glory, was the president of the United States, Franklin D. Roosevelt!

Burning with embarrassment, Aunt Kathryn pulled off the road and let the cars containing the governor, mayor and a scatload of other dignitaries pass by. When she finally reached home she didn't say a word about her terrible day until my Uncle Bill got home from work.

"Kay, you would never guess what happened today. Some dizzy woman got into the president's procession and it took two Secret Service guys and a trooper to get her out! It's a wonder she wasn't shot! The president's guards are so nervous about assassins. They don't ask questions."

"Does anyone know who the woman was?" Aunt Kathryn asked nervously.

"No, she seemed harmless, just confused. They all had a good laugh about it later."

It was many weeks before Aunt Kathryn finally 'fessed up that *she* had been "the dizzy woman" in the story—and it was many months before she drove to the city again. ❖

I Loved That Model T

By Millie O. Wells

It was the mid-1920s, when I was yet a teenager, that I fell in love with my brother's Model T on my father's farm. I had taken many rides with him on those rough wagon trails in North Dakota, but when I asked him if I could drive all by myself, the answer was always a firm "No."

What my brother didn't know was that I had my mind made up to master the technique of driving his car, and every time I rode with him I had a notepad and pencil tucked in my front overall pocket. I wore more overalls than dresses as I loved the outdoors and abhorred the kitchen.

On those rides, whenever I learned something new about the Model T, I surreptitiously jotted myself a note.

I tried different times to just take the car, but my brother's eagle eye was always on me. I was sure the world wasn't coming to an end and I had time to wait for my chance to get into that automobile alone.

I finally had everything lined up to go. I thought I had mastered my lesson on starting the car, but when I gave the crank a turn, not one sound came from the motor. I tried it again—not a single sputter.

My luck finally changed one January day when my brother woke up with the mumps. Boy, was I happy as I went around the house singing *Yankee Doodle* and other songs I had learned in grade school. Then I filled a tin pail with water from the 50-gallon wooden barrel by the kitchen range, heated the water, and carted it to the henhouse for an excuse to get to the car behind the barn.

I heard the kitchen door open behind me and my brother's voice boomed through the crisp morning air. "Ma already took water to the chickens!" Before I could answer, I heard Ma tell him to leave me alone, as I wanted something to do on weekends.

I hurriedly dumped the water into the long wooden trough and dashed out behind the barn to "the old tin can," as Pa called the car.

My hands were numb from cold and I looked at my notepad, but to my dismay I needed hot ashes in sub-zero weather to start the car. These ashes were to be placed under the car toward the front to cheer up the motor, but the ash pan was in the potbellied heater. I walked back to the house like a whipped pup, but although the wheels weren't spinning on the Model T, it wasn't long before the wheels began to rotate in my mind.

That night in bed, I read and reread my notes like I was memorizing a poem for a Christmas program. I had numbered the items. Some were for summer driving—like filling the canvas bag with water and hanging it on the side of the car. "Don't fill water in the radiator or you may get sprayed with a miniature scalding geyser." There were other summertime notes, but the winter ones were what I needed now.

Then I read, "Set a pan of hot ashes beneath the car toward the front." That would be easy, as the potbellied heater and the kitchen range both had hot ashes in their pans. "Then wedge a rock or brick under the tire. Jack up the rear wheel if the car won't start. But be sure to not advance the spark lever too far or you may wind up with a sprained wrist, your thumb pushed against your wrist, or even a broken arm, as too much spark will send the car crank spinning backward."

Also in my notepad I had listed where to find the measuring stick to measure how much gasoline was in the gas tank under the front seat, and the tire irons, tire patches and a pair of scissors.

It wasn't so nice to get a flat tire. I had watched my brother patch them time and again and it took all of half an hour. Half an hour in subzero weather could mean frostbite on these North Dakota plains where the temperature sometimes dropped to 40 below. But then, most everybody stayed home, and especially if there was a lot of snow, the car wasn't used at all.

To fix a flat tire, the wheel with the flat had to be jacked up. A set of tire irons was used to remove the tire from the rim. Then the inner tube was taken from the casing, and the tube scraped and buffed before the round or square patch was glued over the puncture. The tube was then pushed back into the casing and air was pumped into the tube by a hand pump. Pumping took a lot of energy; I knew because I had changed and pumped my brother's tires more than once. All I could do was hope I wouldn't have a flat—if I ever got the Model T started.

The next item on my pad was to keep the running board on the side of the car free from ice and snow to keep from slipping when going into or out of the vehicle.

Also in my notes was a reminder that if the car wouldn't go up a steep hill, just back it up, as it had more power that way—or so my brother had told me. And when going over rough roads, I had watched him put the Model T in low gear. It barely crept over some areas of that countryside.

When I had finally mastered all my notes, I was ready to go to sleep. The next morning found me wide awake as the crisp morning air had chilled my nose and cheeks. I heard Pa shaking down the dead ashes in the potbellied heater and telling Ma that the wind had come up during the night and every speck of coal was burned up. The same thing had happened in the kitchen stove.

After breakfast, I offered to carry the ashes out. Ma sent me to the chicken coop with the dead ashes for the fowl to roll around in. I dumped the ashes inside the henhouse door; most of them fell into the drinking trough. Then I ran back to the house to clean out the hot ashes from the stove before they died out.

I gathered as many of the hot ashes as I could get. When I passed through the shed attached to the house, I grabbed one of Pa's chambray shirts to cover them, but a few seconds later, the shirt began to smoke and quickly caught fire. I walked cautiously to the car and placed the pan of ashes and the burning shirt under the automobile. Then I followed the instructions in my notepad on how to start the car.

I finally had everything lined up to go. I *thought* I had mastered my lesson on starting the car, but when I gave the crank a turn, not one sound came from the motor. I tried it again—not a single sputter. I tried to figure out what was wrong. It was getting colder by the minute. I made another thorough examination and found that the battery was missing. That ended my intentions of driving that day.

When I got back to the house, Mother asked, "What took you so long?"

As I leaned over to warm my hands over the kitchen range, I replied, "Oh, I just looked around the barn to see if the cattle and horses were all right, and the little kittens in the manger." I don't know if she believed me or not, but she let it go at that.

I didn't get to drive that cold winter day. But when summer came, my brother taught me how to drive. He remarked how fast I learned. Since then, I have driven not only a Model T, but other Fords, Oldsmobiles and Pontiacs. My present car is a Ford station wagon. But I still love my memories of the old Model T. ❖

Black Beauty

By Edith G. Oldham

I want to tell you about my favorite car. She wasn't my first. That first car was a used one, a 1941 Chevy coupe. Before the end of our first year together, its engine threw a rod. I had to get a rebuilt motor, which I believe was about $100.

I was only a schoolteacher and I didn't have $100 bills to throw around too often. So my dad located another used car for me and had the salesman bring it to the house to show to me.

When my dad told me he had a car out front, I said I didn't

Black Beauty and me

need one. But when he insisted that I take a trial ride in this auto he had selected, I realized that he sincerely wanted to help me.

The car was a shiny, black 1949 DeSoto sedan, and to me, it looked like new. The salesman drove it around for a few miles. Then he asked me to get behind the wheel.

I fell in love with the DeSoto as soon as I sat behind the steering wheel. The car had "fluid drive" so I wouldn't have to shift gears manually. She had a fan that cooled the interior. The upholstery was like new. This auto was roomy, with a big backseat and large trunk. Among her finest features was a spotlight on the driver's side so the driver could locate address numbers or objects in the dark. I'd never seen a spotlight on a car before.

But what really convinced me was the ease with which this car handled the road—really comfy! Plus, I could take others along for "joy rides," too. I had my first taste of sheer luxury at last!

This sharp-looking marvel became my "Black Beauty"—my stallion, my knight in shining armor, my spaceship, my Pegasus, my magic carpet, my home away from home. What made the deal sweeter was the price: $800. It was incredible—such luxury at a bargain-basement price! I could handle the cost by trading in my first car to lower the total.

The car reminded me of a coal-black cat, contented, purring along with a soft, smooth idle. I kept her for 13 years, and during that time she gave me a million bucks' worth of sunshine, service and serendipity. She took me on trips to Florida and all over my home state. If I'd had a hiding place, that DeSoto would still belong to me! Her nose always pointed home.

Yes, that DeSoto was my very favorite car. The automobiles that followed could not attain the level of pure pleasure I enjoyed with Black Beauty. I felt like a real lady. ❖

The Two Sisters

By Mack Stanley

There was a swell two-story stucco home on North Seventh Street in Fort Smith, Ark., that I passed every-day on my way to Belle Grove School back in 1917. It was a fancy house with a lot of ornamental gimcrackery, a lot of gables, a veranda that embraced it on three sides, and a big red brick chimney on each end. A heavy-gauge iron fence surrounded the property. It was made up of 1-inch vertical bars with spear-like endings on top.

Out behind the house was a large carriage house with groom and servant quarters above. By then, however, the groom and the horses had gone on to other pursuits and greener pastures. This horse-and-buggy building already had been changed into a garage by what we thought was progress. About the only sign remaining of horse-drawn vehicles was one old surrey with a fringe on top, standing deserted and dejected-looking with its tongue hanging down on the floor. The only companion vehicle was a glistening, shiny, black electric car.

Almost every afternoon the two small sisters who lived in this mansion came out in their black-and-white finery and ceremoni-ously drove that sparkling horseless carriage down the driveway, through the iron gate and onto North Seventh Street. They made a right turn and drove up to Garrison Avenue, then east up the main thoroughfare to the Catho-lic church at the top of this main street. Then they wheeled the vehicle north out Thirteenth Street to "E" Street, made a left turn back down to Seventh, and drove back through the gate, back to their mansion, and into the car-riage house. This whole trip took 30 minutes at most, but you could tell that it was the highlight of their day.

As they rode, those little elderly ladies sat up straight and stiff as royalty, like two animated dress-up dolls, prim and starched, rarely bother-ing to look to either side. One held the bar that guided the high, boxy car with sparrowlike attention to it alone. The other sister clung to the door handle with a death grip, as if she thought that if she relaxed, it would all come apart.

Everyone who knew the ladies knew to skedaddle when they saw them coming. Pedestrians knew they were in danger of life and limb if they should get in these sisters' way. Near misses made many strangers jump for their lives. Even the school kids knew that these little old ladies in their silent vehicle always had the right of way, no matter where.

Once, near the intersection of Garrison and Seventh, when a vegetable peddler failed to negotiate his escape from their steady approach at 15 miles an hour, his potatoes, onions, apples and cabbages were scattered from curb to curb around his damaged huckster's hack. Luckily no one was injured, but that did little to dampen sisters' indignation.

The one who wasn't driving was pretty testy. "Good grief!" she exclaimed. "What's the matter with you, my good man? Couldn't you see us coming?" ❖

> *As they rode, those little elderly ladies sat up straight and stiff as royalty, like two animated dress-up dolls, prim and starched, rarely bothering to look to either side.*

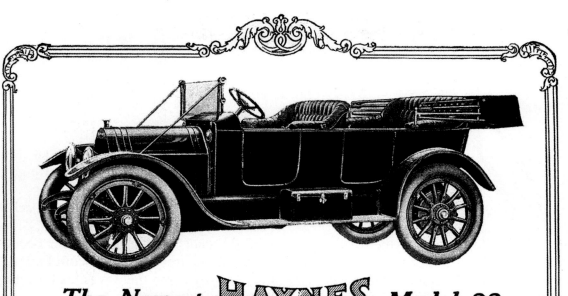

The Newest HAYNES Model 22
Electric Starting and Electric Lighting

FOR the twentieth year of the Haynes Automobile, we announce the complete, perfect
motor car. Haynes Model 22 has every mark of the fine construction that has distin-
guished the Haynes car so many years; it has all the beauty of design that has made
Model 21 so popular; it has such roominess as you never saw in any other automobile; comfort to please those who seek *luxury;* and *an electric starting and electric lighting equipment of
utmost simplicity and absolutely 100 per cent efficiency.*

It is fitting that America's first car—in point of years—should now be America's unques-
tioned *first car* in point of perfect, efficient completeness. And the price for touring car
models is but $2250, f. o. b. factory. We *hope* we shall be able to build enough cars to fill
our dealers' orders.

A Starting Device That is *Not* an Experiment

When so many manufacturers were loudly announcing "self-starters" last year, some
people wondered that we said *nothing* about self-starters. But Haynes owners and Haynes
dealers and everyone else who knew Haynes history did not wonder. *They* knew that when
a *real starting* device was perfected, one that would start a car every time and never allow
any possibility of injury to the motor—*the Haynes would have it.* We were working toward
such a device then, an electric cranking device. It was *perfected* six months ago. But still
we waited. We wanted to be *very sure.* That's Haynes policy. In these six months, the
first Model 22 test cars, equipped with this device, have been put through *thousands* of tests
in the shops and on the road, and the starter has *never* failed.

Hundreds of these tests have been made under unfavorable conditions which could not arise in an owner's
experience, and we couldn't *make* the starter fail. It *cannot* fail. And the equipment is so free from complications, so very simple, that if any trouble ever should appear, the car would *not have to be sent back to the factory.*
Any electrician in America could make wiring repairs on either the motor (starting device), or the dynamo
(lighting device). Consider that point carefully. The average time of 10,000 Model 22 starts has been *5 seconds.*

Need We Speak of Haynes General Construction?

Everyone who knows automobiles at all knows that the Haynes name is a guarantee of the best materials,
correct design, excellent workmanship. Other than for its electric starting and lighting equipment, Model 22
does not differ greatly from the construction of recent Haynes models. The car is roomier. Upholstery *twelve
inches deep* and of fine hair. Motor 4½ x 5½ inches, 40 h. p.; wheel base 120 inches; tires 36 x 4½ inches. Equipment *complete,* including Eisemann dual magneto, Stromberg carburetor, Warner autometer, demountable
rims, top, windshield, etc. You will find the new Model 22 at your Haynes dealer's *now.* Go see it, or write us
for catalog and full details of starting system.

HAYNES AUTOMOBILE COMPANY, 20 Union Street, KOKOMO, INDIANA
1715 Broadway, NEW YORK   510-512 N. Capitol Blvd., INDIANAPOLIS   1702 Michigan Ave., CHICAGO
Van Ness Avenue at Turk Street, SAN FRANCISCO

[1912]

*The two sisters' electric car was from the turn of the 20th century. By 1912 the Haynes electric car had graduated to a more conventional style, complete
with steering wheel.* 1912 Haynes Model 22 ad, House of White Birches nostalgia archives

Woman Driver

By Winifred L. Thompson

My mom was quite a lady. Back in 1922, when I was 12 years old, I took my first automobile ride with my mom.

We lived about 3 miles outside the small city of Olean, N.Y. The streetcar went right by our house on its way to Bradford, Pa. But there had been rumors of the streetcar company abandoning the run to Bradford, so my dad thought we should buy an automobile to get to and from school and work. He worked at the armory in town.

They bought an Overland, a 4-cylinder touring car. Was Dad ever proud of it! He spent half his time at home washing and polishing it.

One sunny, summer day, our car was parked in our long driveway, as we had no garage at that time. Dad still went to work on the streetcar because he hated to get his car dirty on the dirt roads. We lived up in the mountains outside the city. One afternoon, Mom, looking out at the car, said to me, "How would you like to go down to the city with me and pick up your Dad from work?"

Looking at her, dumbfounded, I replied, "You can't drive!"

"Maybe I can't, but I have been watching your father and I think I can," Mom said.

In those days you didn't need to take a driving test or have a driver's license or car insurance. Mom said, "Go get the keys and then climb in and we will take off."

"Not me," I replied. "I don't want to get killed!"

Well, Mom just gave me the kind of look that sends shivers down your back. "Crawl in," she said. "You may bring me luck." So, very meekly and hesitantly, I did as I was told—but I sat in the backseat.

She started with a jerk, which I was afraid had broken my neck. Finally, after a few tries, she learned how to let the clutch out slowly, and by giving it gas very timidly, we got started down the road.

Heaving a big sigh, Mom settled back, both hands clamped on the steering wheel. "This is fun," she said, "nothing to it. I *knew* I could drive."

Well, we drove up to Lincoln Park opposite the post office and there was Dad, waiting for the streetcar to stop.

When Mom honked the horn, Dad looked up and saw us. His mouth fell open and he looked as though he might keel over. He sauntered over to the car and asked, "How the heck did you get down here with my car?"

Mom, looking like the cat that had eaten the canary, answered, "I drove *our* car. Nothing to it. Want a lift home?"

Dad said, "Move over. You have done enough driving for one day. Besides, driving down is some different than driving up and shifting. Now watch me carefully."

Well, after that, Mom would take us downtown for school and work. Then she had the car to herself for the rest of the day.

Once she and I went for a ride and bought ice-cream cones. Coming to a stoplight, and not having signals of any kind, she put her left arm out the window, with her ice-cream cone in her hand, to signal that she was stopping.

A young man, waiting for her to stop and waiting for the light to turn, nonchalantly reached over and took her ice cream out of her hand. He said, "Thanks!" and continued on in front of the car and down the street, licking away on her cone.

Mom was so surprised that she was speechless for a second. Then she burst out laughing as she took her foot off the brake. "I guess he wanted that cone more than I did," she laughed. She always had a great sense of humor. ❖

Life With a Ford

By Florence P. Haynes

I remember the Roaring '20s—and long before that, which is something we won't go into. According to information I can gather, the Ford Motor Company started producing cars in 1908, but it wasn't until 1914 that the Model T made its appearance. Thereby hangs my tale.

We lived on the plains of western Nebraska, and it was a long way to town with the team and wagon. We all knew that Papa had been turning over in his mind the possibility of buying an automobile although he never came right out and said so. He was a sport at heart, and it was hard for him to settle down and face the fact that he had nine children and had to work for a living.

He was a handsome man of German and French descent, with fair skin, deep blue eyes, and a shock of curly black hair. I think he must have realized just how handsome he was.

Papa was smart, too, and a schemer, and I guess the Lord cooperated, for his first three children were boys. They were taught to do a man's work long before they were men. But then Papa missed the boat; he had four girls in a row. Undaunted, however, Papa reasoned that girls might not be a total loss and set about teaching us the rudiments of farm work. Maybe we could do half a man's work—and we did.

> *Uncle Frank and Aunt Agnes unexpectedly drove in one Sunday in their new Model T Ford. After all the oohs and aahs were heard, Papa and Uncle Frank got down to the hard facts of cost and could a working man afford it?*

Now, don't think I'm complaining because we were taught to work. I wish there were more Mammas and Papas today who believed in the saying that mischief finds work for idle hands to do. I'm beginning to ramble again—that seems to be one of my failings—but I'll get back to my story.

The whole thing came to a head when Uncle Frank and Aunt Agnes and their girls unexpectedly drove in one Sunday in their new Model T Ford. After all the *oohs* and *aahs* of disbelief over the miracle of the machine, and after each had been taken for a spin, Papa and Uncle Frank got down to the hard facts. How much did the thing cost, how economical was it to run, and could a working man afford it?

Strangely enough, I wasn't too interested in all of these details. All I could think of was the glorious feeling of riding in the backseat with my head leaned back on the cushions and my eyes closed. I seemed to be floating. *Surely this must be what heaven would be like!*

How well I remember that Sunday evening. With the chores done and supper over, the talk just naturally turned to the Model T. Maybe Papa thought Mama would be more receptive with a full stomach—and Papa could be quite tactful when the need arose. Wouldn't it be nice to make that weekend trip to town to deliver produce in comfort? he argued. "Think of the occasional literary we attended. It would be so much nicer for the children." (Not that we needed any persuading, especially my teenaged brothers.) It looked like we were going to have a good crop year and cattle were a good price, so what did Mama think about it?

Always conservative, Mama dissented, which was the wrong thing to do. With a blood-curdling howl, Papa brought his fist down on the big dining table where we always gathered for such family consultations, and announced that it was about time he exercised his rights as head of the house. If his baby brother with only girls to help with the work could afford an automobile, he guessed we could.

We children all cringed at his outburst and wondered what would happen next, but when he announced that we would get the auto, we nodded in agreement that Papa was right; the man *should* be the one to make the decisions. We straightened up in our chairs and gazed at Papa with admiration.

Mama didn't need to straighten up. She had sat straight as an arrow throughout the ordeal without batting an eye. Mama was a brave woman; Papa didn't scare *her!* But he was a sport, all right, and not to be outdone by his little brother. The voice of authority had spoken and that was that. We knew that when it came right down to it, poor Mama didn't stand a chance.

Next morning, bright and early, found Papa rattling down the road toward town with the double box wagon and the team of mules. That evening when he got home, the wagon was piled high with new lumber, a keg of nails and a bucket of red paint. At the supper table he announced that the new Model T touring car had been ordered, complete with side curtains, and would be delivered in a few weeks. We children tried to conceal our excitement to spare Mama's feelings. We knew she wanted the car, but Mama was the one who always schemed and planned to make ends meet and she was apprehensive.

None the less, as the days passed and the new garage took shape, some of our enthusiasm rubbed off on her, and by the time the last coat of paint was on, Mama was almost as eager as the rest of us. She was still worried, though. How could Papa get the car home when he had never driven one?

Papa informed her that was no problem. The dealer had promised to take him out for a drive and show him all the gadgets and their functions. There was really nothing to it.

The long-awaited day finally arrived, and according to plan, Papa rode to town with a neighbor to bring the new car home. Before leaving, however, we were all told over and over to watch, and when we saw him coming, to open the barbed-wire gate at the road and then the garage doors, and above all, stay out of the way. That car was going to receive the best of care; no sitting out in the weather.

I doubt that a longer day ever existed. We all took turns watching the road, which was visible for miles in that flat prairie country. Long before sundown, a shriek from my brother alerted us that Papa was coming. It couldn't be anyone else. No one out our way had a car, and the fog

Seven people in a Model T touring car was not uncommon in the Good Old Days. When you had a car, you had plenty of friends!

of dust was moving much too rapidly to be a team.

He was right, for after what seemed like an eternity, Papa was near enough to be recognizable in that shining black beauty. As instructed, the boys opened the gate and the garage doors. Then we all lined up along the drive to witness the grand entry. Mama held onto the two little boys and kept cautioning the rest of us to "Stand back, stand back!" Papa wasn't a very experienced driver yet.

Truer words were never spoken! In sailed Papa, cocky as the sport he imagined himself to be, through the gate, through the garage doors and, with a deafening crash, right on through the back end of the garage.

The next scene I won't undertake to describe. Parts of it wouldn't do to print anyway. I know we were all warned in no uncertain terms what would happen if we mentioned this to a soul, but some

We all learned to crank Papa's Model T, but this photograph is set up. Little ones didn't crank because it might kick back and could easily break a small child's arm.

way the news leaked out and for weeks, Papa was deluged with anonymous picture postcards depicting the Model T Ford and its idiosyncrasies. Suffice it to say, no one but Papa was ever allowed to touch the steering wheel of that car.

When it came to cranking the fool thing, that was a different matter. We all became quite good at that. What I am trying to say is that I had never learned to drive, which leads me up to the Roaring '20s. (As I said, I am prone to ramble.)

I met my husband in the spring of 1927, and in August of that same year, we were married. Don't tell him I said so, but it may have been that snappy little black Model T coupe that first attracted me. However, after all those years and five children, I'm sure there was more to it than that.

All that summer, during our courtship, I had been begging John (my husband-to-be) to teach me to drive Betsy, which we had fondly named the little coupe. I had saved from my meager earnings and bought pink silk bengaline to make draw curtains for the back and side windows. Nothing like privacy. And besides, they were all the rage with the younger set in the 1920s, along with the marcelle and the Charleston. I envisioned myself as the envy of all the neighborhood girls as I flitted up and down the road in the little black coupe with the pink silk curtains. A few times I persuaded him to let me under the wheel, but it seemed he had his mind on anything but teaching me to drive, so I finally gave up the idea. Secretly, I vowed that once we were married, I would teach myself to drive whenever the opportunity presented itself.

We settled on a little farm about a mile down a winding prairie road from where John's sister lived. On this lovely September morning, Hubby was called to a neighbor's to assist with some farm work and I had the day to myself.

All of a sudden, the idea struck: *This* was the day I had been waiting for! I would drive down the trail and spend the day with my sister-in-law. I breezed through my morning work and in no time was into a clean house-dress and ready for a lark.

The radiator was checked for water; we had filled the gas tank on our last trip to town, so that was no problem. Once again I familiarized myself with the various pedals and levers and, remembering what each one was for, I felt ready for anything.

I was in a festive mood. "Reckless" might describe it better in light of what happened later. This modern buggy had a self-starter and one try was all it took. If memory serves me right, the procedure was to release the emergency brake, step on the low pedal, pull down on the gas lever, and you were off with a roar. The more practice you had, the more adept you became, but I was still a novice. I had to admit that I started with a jerk, but there was nothing wrong with my sacroiliac—yet.

Back then, a typical country road on the prairie consisted of two ruts spaced the proper distance apart to accommodate a vehicle. It meandered across the prairie in whatever direction the original traveler had felt like going at the moment, usually the shortest distance between two points. This particular road did its meandering along a barbed-wire fence. As the Model T and I rattled merrily along with the windows rolled down to catch the warm summer breeze, I was totally happy. I wondered why I had waited so long; there was nothing to this business of driving a car.

Then, just as I was about to pat myself on the back, it happened.

Now, I love all of God's creatures, but a grasshopper is one thing I like better a long way off rather than down the back of my neck. Grant you, there are better ways to drive a car than with both hands behind your back your legs wound around the steering column like a pretzel, and eyes focused heavenward. (I was more agile in those days.) The next thing I knew, Betsy gave one last desperate leap and came to a dead stop, her hind wheels crossways of the ruts and her front ones astride the barbed-wire fence. I never really knew *what* happened to the grasshopper.

Meekly I crawled out to survey the damage. I wasn't so sure about my sacroiliac now. Only three fenceposts were down, though the wire had been pulled from that many more, and I found I could still navigate, although a bit painfully.

Well, nothing to do but repair the damage, and John need be none the wiser. Another try with the starter and after a few coughs, sputters and groans of protest at such rough treatment, Betsy took off and purred like a kitten.

It didn't take long to get home once I got her disengaged from the barbed wire. She had the rest of the day to lick her wounds (of which I was unaware at the time) and recuperate, while I, armed with posthole diggers, wire stretchers, hammer and staples, spent my day digging post-holes and repairing the fence as good as new. Bless Papa for having taught me the fundamentals of fence building.

When John got home that evening, I had prepared his favorite meal and wore my most bewitching and innocent smile—until I saw his face. One look and I knew he was aware that something had happened. But how could he possibly know? Only Betsy and I shared the secret. Rattlesnakes and jackrabbits just don't carry tales.

With nary a word, I was invited outside to explain the three barbed-wire scratches that ran the full length of Betsy's right side. In my concern over the fence, I had missed them.

After a lot of explaining and apologizing, all was forgiven. Newlyweds have a way of kissing and making up, you know. On future trips I was accompanied by John until I became as proficient as he was, although he would never admit it, I'm sure.

I still enjoy driving, only now the automatic transmission, power brakes and power steering make it a lot easier. John sometimes thinks my foot gets a little heavy on the accelerator, but I don't think 40 miles an hour is too fast, do you? Especially for an experienced driver like myself. ❖

The Puddle Jumper

By Madeline Huss

Long before any of the other mothers in town even thought of such a thing as driving, mine traversed the roads in her beloved 1926 Model T Ford. My brother and I were fortunate to accompany her on her travels in what she fondly called "the Puddle Jumper," so named for the car's ability to navigate rain-soaked dirt roads without bogging down in the mud.

Mama taught herself to drive by climbing into the seat of her brother John's pickup truck when he wasn't looking and practicing shifting until she gained the confidence to ask him to take her for her driver's test.

"You'll never pass!" he said. "It will only be a waste of time." But Mama persisted until he drove her to the Motor Vehicle Agency.

When she completed the test, she walked over to where John waited and waved her new license in his face. He shook his head. "What's this world coming to," he wondered aloud, "when they let a woman drive on the road?"

Mama decided she needed a car of her own. But she and my father were newlyweds saving to buy a house; finding money to buy an automobile seemed impossible. However, she solved the dilemma by offering to drive other people to take their driver's tests for a small fee. It took a long time, but eventually she was able to buy a used Model T. It became her well-loved Puddle Jumper.

The car was still in excellent condition when my brother and I came along a few years later. Its black exterior shone like new, thanks to Mama's tender loving care. Every Saturday, when we were old enough, we helped her wash the Puddle Jumper, then carefully dry it off with old rags while she applied the wax.

Daddy never learned to drive. He was content to sit next to her, acting as navigator, when we went for our Sunday-afternoon rides.

During bad weather, Mama used to drive Daddy to work at the bleachery to save him the 2-mile walk. I remember the time when the weatherman on our Philco radio kept predicting that a hurricane was headed our way.

The rain fell steadily all day long. Mama looked out the window. Even though it was only 4 o'clock, the dark skies made it seem much later. Rain sheeted against the house, and the two big trees out front swayed with the wind until the topmost branches nearly touched the ground. I shivered as my brother, who stood next to Mama, pointed to the sky. "Look, green lightning!" I'd never seen green lightning.

I heard a *craaack* as a large branch broke off the tree and lay across the yard. Mama reached for her purse. "Where are you going?" I asked as she put on her raincoat.

"To get your father, of course! He'll never make it walking in this weather."

"In the Puddle Jumper?" I couldn't believe she'd try to drive while green lightning streaked across the sky.

But she nodded. "You children behave while I'm gone. I won't be long."

My brother and I started to cry. "Don't leave us alone! Let us come with you!"

Mama thought for a moment, then said, "You may as well. I'll only worry about leaving you. The Puddle Jumper will make the trip without any problem, you'll see." She sounded calm but I could see a troubled look in her eyes.

Mama drove down the road, peering intently through the windshield, trying to see where she was going. My brother and I sat quietly in the backseat, almost too afraid to breathe and disturb her concentration. The wind threatened to toss the car to the side of the road. Still, Mama was able to steer around fallen branches and downed power lines. With a sigh of relief, we saw the building where Daddy worked. Mama pulled up in front and Daddy, who'd been standing right outside the door, ran over and got in.

"Thank goodness you're here," he said. "You shouldn't have come out in this, but I'm glad you did!" We made it home all right, even through places where the water had risen almost 2 feet.

Yes, Mama was always there for us, to drive us in her beloved Puddle Jumper. ❖

My First Car

By Cornelia Mol Gruys

*I*n 1939 it was somewhat unusual for an 18-year-old young lady to own a car. Our family farm was experiencing hard times, coming through the Depression and the drought in Minnesota. Nevertheless, Pa bought the black 1930 Model A Ford coupe for me for $100. I would pay him back from the money I made at my first teaching job, beginning that fall. But my salary was $45 a month, so it would take a while.

Pa taught me to drive going around and around in our mowed alfalfa field. Finally I was ready to take the car out on my own. It was a warm day in the middle of August. Preparations had to be made before the first day of school.

My two-room country school, District 16, near the small town of Silver Creek, was about 5 miles from our farm. It felt great to be driving the car by myself for the first time.

The hours at school flew by and I needed to hurry home to help Ma prepare dinner for our threshing crew. I gathered books and papers to work on at home, then placed them on the little shelf behind the front seat. Cars did not have air conditioning then, so I had both windows wide open.

Breezing along at 35 miles per hour, I was feeling pretty proud and excited about my car. Then some of the papers began blowing out of the window on the passenger side. I reached over to turn up the window, and the next thing I knew, the car had tipped over on its right side into a ditch. In disbelief, I managed to crawl out. Then I felt my aching back where the loose top of the seat had smacked me.

This is the only picture taken of me with my first car, a 1930 black Model A Ford coupe. Ma took the photograph at our farm shortly before I sold the car in June 1943.

No one came by on the country road so I walked to a neighbor's farm to call home. Soon Pa and his threshing crew of eight showed up. In a few minutes they had righted my car. Of course, I had to endure a lot of teasing and joking.

How humiliating and humbling! Despite the battery acid spilling onto the seat and ruining the upholstery, and despite several nasty dents in its side, Pa declared my car was fit for me to drive home.

"Oh no, not me!" I bawled.

"Oh yes, you!" Pa said. "If you don't drive it right now, you'll have time to get yourself worked up and scared. You get in and drive it home. I'll be driving close behind you in my car."

I wondered what good that would do me. Then, with all those threshers standing around trying to convince me, Pa continued, "I've known people, especially women, who never drove again after an accident." Though I protested loudly, Pa was still boss.

In the many years since, I have met women like those Pa mentioned. They have told me it was true. Thanks to a wise father, not only did I drive my car home alone that day, but the accident taught me to drive carefully with great respect for the power of a vehicle.

And thanks also to my Heavenly Father, each of my four children learned the same lesson. As young drivers, through minor mishaps with no serious injuries, they became careful drivers, too.

My dear little car was tenderly undented and fixed almost as good as new by Pa. Hour after hour he worked on it, never complaining. For days I complained about my aching back, so Pa took me to a farmer friend who knew how to "adjust" backs. One visit cured my complaints, but sometimes I think I still feel the spot, although I don't blame the car.

I didn't give my car a name, probably because I had so many nicknames. Recently I showed these old pictures to my brother, Chris. He said, "Hey, I remember putting the hood ornament on your car for you." How blessed I was to have such a family!

I lived at home during the four years I taught at the school. The upper-grade teacher, Myrtle Krause, roomed and boarded at our home and rode with me.

While Ma made breakfast and packed a lunch for us, Pa and Chris would start my car and back it out of the shed. Often they had to shovel snow to get it out. Sometimes they used a homemade snowplow and horses to make a path in the driveway for my car, Myrtle and me.

I can't remember my dear little car giving us trouble. To get gas, I'd drive into the tiny town of Silver Creek where my uncle, Bill Mol, owned the only gas station and garage. Uncle Bill would always say, "I'll go to work and keep her in tiptop shape for you." And he did.

Not only did I love my dear little car, I also loved teaching "the little-room kids," as they were called. On especially nice days we would have art and poetry classes outdoors by the lake.

Once the children suggested they would love to visit our family farm, which bordered two beautiful lakes, Sugar Lake and Indian Lake. Their parents approved of our plans.

Lunches and goodies for the day were packed and stored in my car's trunk. Like a mother duck leading her ducklings, I drove my car as the children followed.

Two or three at a time, they took turns riding in the car with me. In those days we had very few discipline problems and the country roads did not have much traffic. At our farm, Ma greeted us on that warm spring day with cool drinks and more treats.

For weeks after that expedition, we used our experiences to write stories. We found the names for the wildflowers we had gathered and for leaves we had pressed. My little car was often mentioned in their stories and conversations.

From time to time I meet some of my former pupils at church functions in Silver Creek. They tell me how their grandchildren ask to hear stories about "the Good Old Days." Then we reminisce and laugh as we recall those wonderful memories. And still remembered is the old Ford coupe.

In the spring of 1943, during World War II, the time came to say goodbye to beloved pupils and sell my dear little car. I was leaving Minnesota to go to California to marry my childhood sweetheart. When we were children, he had attended District 16, while I went to a country school near our farm. We met at the church where our grandparents and parents were members. My trip to California had to be by train because gasoline and tires were rationed.

If you remember wartime prices and you will not be surprised that my car sold for $200, a tremendous profit.

Now my three sons and some of my grandchildren are antique- and classic-car buffs and collectors. So far, though, none of them has a 1930 Model A Ford coupe.

It would be a thrill to have my picture taken again beside a car exactly like my old one. Since I am an antique too, such a picture would show a good example of a pair of classics! ❖

How Not to Drive a Car

By Norma S. Archer

1938 *Farmer's Wife*, House of White Birches nostalgia archives

*W*hen I see how anxious kids are to drive today, I chuckle, remembering how I had to be pushed into it at 18—and much against my will.

After graduating from high school during the Depression, I got a job at $20 a week, a sum many families were living on in those lean years. But not realizing my good fortune, I happily blew most of my salary on a smart new wardrobe because Mom had always bought my clothing too large so I could "grow into it."

Dad, who owned and ran a car-repair shop, quickly halted my joyride when he discovered I had worked a whole year and had saved nothing! "You should be ashamed of yourself!" he scolded.

A few days later, he informed me, "Norma, I have a nice little car in the shop that I will fix up and sell to you for $65. And I'll teach you how to drive!" I stared at him, aghast, but as you didn't dare argue with your parents in those days, I knew I was stuck with it.

Soon, Dad took me out in the family car, drove to a nearby dam and stopped at its base. "Now, watch what I do," he said. He started the car, shifted, accelerated and circled the area. Returning to the starting point, he stopped. "Now you do it," he told me, getting out of the car so I could slide into the driver's seat.

Shaking with fear, I moved over, but I couldn't think of a single thing to do. "Put your foot on the starter," he said. I did. "Now shift into first and let the clutch out."

I did that, too.

"Now release the brake and start moving."

We moved, but I kept looking at my feet until Dad yelled, "Look where you're going!" I looked up to see that I was veering off the road. "Put on the brake!" he shouted. I hit the accelerator.

By the time we got home, I was crying, Dad was mad, and we weren't speaking.

What to do? I *had* to learn to drive—but not with Dad, I resolved. However, neighbors I talked to were delighted to show me the basics. I became more confident and popular—"Boy, she has her own car!"

Then my friend's college math teacher, Peter, took over. Dad had emphasized, "Don't go too fast; if you hit something, it won't be as bad."

But Peter kept saying. "Go faster, go faster," and I did—until I ran into the car ahead of me! Peter then told me, "Keep quiet and let me do the talking."

But when the driver came over, despite Peter's scowling face, I sobbed, "I'm just learning to drive." My tears must have moved the man, because after examining his car and finding no damage, he graciously let us go on our, albeit slower, way.

I decided to take some professional lessons. The teacher showed me exactly what to do and how to do it. When I became upset, he would let me park until I calmed down. Soon, he told me I was ready for my driving test.

I wore an open-back sundress on the broiling-hot summer day my driver's test was scheduled, but my back was still soaked with perspiration. As I entered my small Chevy with the rumble seat, the stout inspector said, "I'm not here to scare you," and I relaxed a little.

I drove to the top of the steep hill with a stop sign without sliding back, but when I turned the car around on a side street, it bucked wildly. Laughing self-consciously, I said, "This car has a bucking clutch—ha, ha." The inspector made no comment. *My goose is cooked,* I thought. But it wasn't; I got my license in three days.

Still, the things others seemed to find easy were hard for me. As I parked the car in our driveway, I hit the house! I couldn't parallel-park no matter how hard I tried. Driving through a narrow gate with stone pillars on each side, the door handle got caught and the windshield shattered.

After my father died, I *had* to drive, since Mom didn't. She and I especially enjoyed traveling together because we could take our time. Dad had seldom stopped, even for dire necessities.

When my sister got her license, I happily relinquished my post, and I have driven as little as possible since. But I still am the proud owner of a driver's license, used mostly for identification rather than its original purpose—which probably makes the highways a lot safer for us all. ❖

© *From Seasons Past* by John Sloane

Out For a Spin

Chapter Three

*J*anice and I have a favorite picnic spot along the
creek that runs through the middle of our property.
The creek meanders east of the old home place
that Janice's grandmother homesteaded just after
the turn of the 20th century. The chimney of the cabin
Grandma and Grandpa Barnes built now stands like a
lone sentinel guarding the site.

Janice loves the spot because it takes her back to her roots. She is
reminded of her Grandma Katie, who died when Janice was a little girl.
When Janice was young and her father worked in the hay fields along
the creek bottoms, it was a spot to rest in the shade of the sycamores
after bringing the men water or lunch. Then she could watch the hay-
stacks grow, pick wildflowers or dangle her feet in a cool pool of spring
water. All of those memories crowd in whenever we picnic there.

I too am taken back to my roots with a visit to the little picnic
spot. For me, however, it reminds me when, on Sunday afternoons
after church, Daddy said to Mama and us kids, "Why don't we go out
for a spin?"

"Out for a spin" was more than a Sunday drive for us. Mama packed
a picnic and we all piled into the car for the trip. It seemed so far in
those days, but I realized later that it wasn't over 10 miles or so. In the
Good Old Days just going "out for a spin" was enough; the picnic was
icing on the cake.

Part of the way the road was paved, but soon Daddy turned onto a
gravel road that gradually became no more than a path. We squeaked to
a stop at the base of a huge oak tree. There Mama and my sister Donna
unfolded a quilt that was our table and began laying out the bounty: fried
chicken, rolls, potato salad, beans, apple cider. There was no paper plates
or plasticware back in those days, so we had to take our normal kitchen
utensils with us for the meal. Still, somehow Mama was able to squeeze
it all into two large baskets.

Meanwhile we menfolk scouted the best fishing spots. Hopefully the
return trip home would be with bass for the supper table. Then it was
back to the shade of the giant oak for victuals and a short nap before the
serious fishing commenced. If the fish were biting, our interest was keen.
If not, we were as likely to content ourselves with games of hide-and-
seek or tag.

As shadows lengthened we gathered up the remnants of a perfect
day, loaded back into our old car and spun our way back home, tired
but content. I think it's about time I loaded Janice up and took her to my
favorite picnic spot from the Good Old Days. I'll choose some beautiful
Sunday afternoon, and we'll go out for a spin.

—Ken Tate

John Slobodnik

Sunday Drives

By Helen M. Rawlings

Remember how Sunday drives were almost a ritual back in the Good Old Days? At our house it was nigh a weekly event that carried the entire family on adventures never to be forgotten.

Our first car was a Chandler; I remember little about it. But the next one, a Willys Knight, was a memorable conveyance that transported us on many thrilling explorations throughout the countryside. It was a two-seated touring car with leather seats and a compartment below the backseat that held the snap-on curtains with isinglass portholes that we attempted to apply if inclement weather occurred. More than once, the rain had stopped by the time the curtains were in place and my father would be drenched because all the snap fasteners were on the outside. The driver had to manipulate by hand the only windshield wiper, which was on his or her side of the windshield.

Sometimes a picnic was scheduled at a choice spot along a shallow, clear stream where we could remove our shoes and stockings and wade. The fine sand and pebbles were clearly visible through the water, and collecting pebbles of a certain color was like mining gold. When my father took his fishing pole along, we knew we would only be permitted to sit on the bank and let our toes dangle in the water. Wading would scare the fish away.

Once, near a creek, we came to a screeching halt. A mother duck, marching like a drill sergeant, defiantly led her brood single file in front of us.

Our picnic area had a beautiful cold spring spilling out from a cluster of rocks. It could only be reached by following a nearby railroad track and walking on the ties over a precariously high railroad bridge over the stream. If we had become dizzy and lost our footing, we could have been killed if we fell on the rocks below, or knocked unconscious and drowned! We often wondered what we would do if a train approached while we were on the bridge. Just one excursion over to the spring along with the return trip carrying a container of ice-cold water promptly scared us enough that we were glad to comply with our parents' suggestion that we select some other source of amusement.

Road maps and directions were unnecessary. My father, being fond of hunting, fishing and hiking, was thoroughly acquainted with the countryside and knew where every road would lead us. Back then, roadbeds were dirt or crushed rock, and in dry weather our car created a cloud of dust. If another car approached, we could tell well in advance if he was driving fast from the size of the dust cloud the car created. As we passed the speeding car, its wheels threw pebbles and gravel against ours, and the wind carried the dust over the fields, coating the foliage. Of course, the dust blew on and into our open car, making it necessary to clean it after every outing.

It was always a contest to see who would spy the first red-winged blackbird or meadowlark. Sometimes we tried to count how many we saw during the entire excursion. Once, near a creek, we came to a screeching halt. A mother duck, marching like a drill sergeant, defiantly led her brood single file in front of us. Dad never drove fast because the outings were a learning experience as well as an opportunity to drink in all the beauty of the countryside.

At different seasons of the year, the directions in which we drove had definite purpose. In early spring, we watched for pussywillows. In a shaded, sheltered area carpeted with violets, sweet williams and jack-in-the-pulpit, we picked generous bouquets, which partially wilted on the drive home. Sometimes in the ditches along the road-side we'd find black-eyed susans, wild tiger lilies and delicate wild pink roses.

The driver had to manipulate by hand the only windshield wiper, which was on his or her side of the windshield.

In early autumn, we always headed for the farm of our parents' friends who had an enormous apple orchard. A fruit cellar had been constructed under an adjoining hill and the entrance was reinforced on all sides with rocks. It was always exciting to follow the grownups inside the dark cavern where Mother selected by lantern light the bushel basket of fruit she preferred.

Years later, we were saddened when a paved highway replaced the gravel road and, in the widening, destroyed that productive and beautiful orchard and most of the farm buildings.

Another direction took us into some rolling wooded hills. Here, if no one had preceded us, we filled our gunnysacks with black walnuts, butternuts and hickory nuts in a short time. "Going nutting," as we called it, was great fun, but we hated to think of the tedious hours we would later spend picking the meats from the shells. Dad placed the filled sacks on the wide running boards against the fenders and drove home more slowly than we had come to avoid jarring the cargo loose.

Cattails and milkweed pods were more treasures we sought in autumn. Mondays found us taking them to school where our teachers put them on display in the schoolroom.

Sometimes pheasants would surprise us by flying dangerously close to the windshield on their flight from a cornfield. Near farmhouses, chickens always seemed to be roaming the dirt roads, squawking in fright as we approached and darting first one way and then the other. For a very long time, automobiles seemed to be a curiosity or a source of annoyance to farmers' dogs. Most of them raced to the road and barked wildly as they attempted to stay abreast of the car as it passed. It seemed a miracle that they escaped being caught under the wheels.

Riding through the beautiful farm country enabled us to learn the names of different kinds of cattle and hogs. Sometimes we noted how the animals grouped together and sought the shady places. On one occasion, my parents became quite disturbed when they saw that a herd of cattle had broken through a fence and into a green cornfield where they were eating ravenously and breaking down the cornstalks. Dad immediately turned the car around and drove back to that farmer's house to alert him.

Another farmyard had some goats. Having read a particularly moving animal story about a goat, we dubbed the most personable one "Billy Whiskers," after the hero in the book.

But the world we grew up in has disappeared.

Paved highways, interstates and freeways have made driving anyplace faster and cleaner, but they also deprived people of a rich and wonderful Sunday-afternoon experience. It may be considered old-fashioned, but this joy can be recaptured if folks are willing to drive somewhat out of their way and deeper into the countryside. A wealth of color and wonders are waiting to greet them, along with sunsets, scenes and smells that will linger in their memories forever. ❖

Finding the Sun

By Harriet Tracy DeLong

"Uncle Joe! Oh, stop! *Stop!* I see a rhinoceros!"

Our Model A shuddered to an abrupt halt. My usually unflappable uncle fumbled first with the choke and then the starter. Aunt Ethel's shoulders shook with laughter.

"Oh, honey," she said, "that's just a big, black bull." While Uncle Joe regained control of the Ford, she gently explained to me that a bull was a boy cow.

You see, I was a sophisticated 9-year-old, fresh from the canyons of New York City. I had climbed the Statue of Liberty and had ridden to the top of the Empire State Building. I had seen elephants at Barnum & Bailey's Circus and wandered down the paths of the city zoo. On a school excursion, I had visited a modern dairy farm, but I had never seen a bull.

I'll always remember that introduction to Sunday drives along the back roads of rural northern California.

"Where shall we go today?" was the inevitable question as we three strolled home from church.

"Where we can find the sun," said Aunt Ethel. Eureka's skies were usually covered with a gray layer of clouds blown in from the Pacific Ocean.

"Lawrence Creek!" I'd shout. It was my favorite place.

To get to Lawrence Creek we drove out of town past a romantic white house that stood beside a lily pond with a gazebo in the middle of it. Further on, we examined herds of cattle grazing in the lowlands surrounding Humboldt Bay. Packed in the backseat were the plant press, the binoculars, the wicker picnic basket and the green plaid car robe. Permanent inhabitants of the trunk included car tools, a shovel and pick, and two wooden chocks, very handy when attacking steep, muddy grades.

At the foot of the hill, Uncle Joe shifted into low gear for the 10-mile climb through the woods to Kneeland Prairie. (Any natural opening in the redwoods is a prairie, according to Californians.) Across Kneeland's sunny grassland, my botanist uncle drove slowly. His eyes darted from the dirt road to the unfenced fields, where an interesting plant might catch his attention.

Aunt Ethel and I watched for seven white horses, then searched for a load of hay so we could make a wish. Very rarely could we find that other magical combination of good fortune—a white mule and a redheaded girl.

Just beyond the one-room school where Aunt Ethel used to teach, the road plunged 3 miles down the hill by a series of hair-raising switchbacks to Lawrence Creek. That was more exciting than any ride on a Coney Island roller coaster.

Beside the covered bridge that spanned the shady creek, we parked, spread out the car robe, and munched on homemade bread, cheese and fruit. We made a game of naming 10 trees, 10 shrubs and 10 flowers within sight of our picnic spot. Uncle Joe and I built the "waterworks." I chased small crabs hiding in the rocky bottom or fish flitting through the deeper pools. Aunt Ethel, armed with binoculars for bird watching, settled onto a sunny patch of grass. Uncle Joe spent a peaceful hour collecting flowers and spreading them between the blotters in his plant press.

At dusk we left the creek and chugged slowly up the hill. As we crossed the prairie, we watched the sun settle into the ocean of billowy clouds that clung to the coastline. Wrapped in the car robe, I put my head on Aunt Ethel's shoulder and slept my way through the forest and into the fog.

I'll never forget those days when a kindly aunt and uncle took charge of a bewildered little city girl. Sunday drives introduced me to lambs frisking on a hillside, a calf butting his mother's side for the last drop of milk, and knobby-kneed colts racing the length of a pasture.

Once, after weeks of searching, we finally achieved my greatest ambition. I saw a rooster crow!

It's been more than 60 years since I spied that "rhinoceros." Whenever I tire of gray coastal skies, I feel an irresistible urge to pack the old wicker basket with apples and cheese, throw the faded green robe into the back of the car, and head out to find the sun. ❖

Surrey With the Fringe on Top

By Erma Fajen MacFarlane

"Ducks and geese and chicks better scurry; when I take you out in my surrey. …"

I wasn't taken a-courtin' in one. By the time I was old enough to accept dates, the Model T Ford had long been in use. I do, however, remember many who did their courting in one, and others whose "Just Married" ride into wedded bliss was in a surrey with fringe on top. And I have many happy memories of riding in our own family surrey.

My early years were spent on a farm a mile from town. I lived with my parents, brother and three sisters. The surrey was our primary means of transportation for Sundays and special occasions, while the farm wagon was for weekday use. My father was still using horses when some of our more affluent neighbors were driving cars. My father did not take readily to modern conveniences and conveyances. Therefore, we depended on our faithful horses, Sam and Daisy, to draw the carriage on Sunday, and our other horses pulled the farm wagon and plows.

But even at that time, driving a matched pair of spirited horses hitched to a shiny surrey with fringe on top was nothing to be ashamed of. Some of our neighbors had only heavy wagons for Sunday driving. Yes, we were proud of our shiny surrey with the lovely fringe!

I can still remember Sunday mornings of that era. All dressed in our Sunday best, we climbed proudly into the surrey. Father and my brother helped the "womenfolk" take their seats. Father, Mother and my brother rode in the front seat and we girls sat in the back. Father did the driving until my brother reached the age when he was allowed to take over the reins.

In good weather, this Sunday-morning drive to church was greatly enjoyed by all. In bad weather, however, it was a different story, for then our country road, like most others of that time, could become hazardous. Sometimes we were forced to turn back and miss Sunday school and church. Fortunately, this didn't happen often.

Upon reaching church, our team was tied to the hitching rack provided for that purpose. Other teams and vehicles similar to ours were tied nearby. Little by little, began to make their appearance, and fewer teams were used.

After church was over we usually drove straight home unless we had been invited to eat dinner at the home of friends. This was often the case, and just as often, we had friends share Sunday dinner with us. The town folks especially liked coming out to the farm for a noontime meal. Eating in restaurants was almost unheard of except on very special occasions.

Once in a while we would drive to the local ice plant and buy a large chunk of ice, which had been well wrapped. Then, in midafternoon, we would make ice cream. Mother and my sisters got it ready for the freezer. This was a rare treat for the children. Our parents enjoyed it too, of course, but to the younger children it was very special indeed. Sometimes there was homemade cake, too. Never since has ice cream tasted so good!

One of our cherished treasures is a photo of our family seated in the surrey. We are all dressed in our Sunday best, and Mother's costume is finished off with a lovely hat, as hats for women were very much in vogue in those days. Her face is beaming in that photo. No doubt she was thinking what a fine family she had, and how proud she was of them.

My twin sister and I (the babies) were 4 years old at the time. We were dressed alike in white embroidered dresses with matching bonnets. I'm not sure this type of bonnet was the "in" thing at that time, but at least they kept our hair from blowing as we were riding.

We once took a long trip in our surrey—at least it was considered long in those days. We drove from our home at Rich Hill, Mo., to the still smaller town of Cole Camp, about 90 miles away. We spent the first night at Clinton. The one hotel in Clinton was not exactly first-class, mother later told me.

The cherished photograph of my family in our surrey with the fringe on top.

We were favored with good weather for the entire trip, and had no problems except for one little incident, when the front part of the vehicle became detached from the main part. The horses trotted merrily down the road with the wagon tongue between them, leaving us behind. We were surprised! Mother tried to keep her composure, but we children thought it extremely funny. My father and brother jumped from the carriage and stopped the runaway horses. A quick repair was made to the carriage and soon we were on our way again.

Sam and Daisy, our faithful team, are long gone, and the destiny of the surrey is unknown. I hope it has been restored and has found a place of honor in some museum for vehicles from another era. But I still enjoy fond memories of what a special ride you could have in it every time I hear that little tune from *Oklahoma*. ❖

Burma Shave Signs

By Bob Loeffelbein

Motorists all over the byway scene of America were saddened by the demise of an old friend, the Burma Shave sign. The purveyors of these roadside reminders that had delighted past generations decided to update their advertising campaign. That meant a change from their spot commercials of the billboard world to spot commercials on television. And with that change, another cherished piece of Americana passed into history.

For years these miniature billboard quips had been a joy to the tired traveler, and, always tasteful, they never let their comic rejoinders get out of hand. Consider this example from the early files that was seen briefly beside the road and then removed because of complaints:

Listen birds,
These signs cost money,
So roost awhile,
But don't get funny.
Burma Shave.

After that, no matter how clever or appealing, no jingle was used that might offend anyone—politically, racially, or in any other way. It is for such reasons that you have never seen the following one, either:

If wifie shuns
Your fond embrace,
Don't shoot the iceman,
Feel your face.
Burma Shave

It was September 1926, when the first jingle went up along the side of a road, on U.S. Highway 65, near Lakeville, Minn. Its message was simple and to the point:

Cheer up, face. The war is over! Burma Shave.

Not too inspirational or clever perhaps, but "mighty oaks from little acorns grow," so it wasn't long until there were more than 7,000 sets of these merry jingles lining highways across 43 states.

The actual count of the number of jingles used since 1926 has been lost, but it runs into the multiple thousands. The number that have been rejected that were sent in from the public for consideration runs into millions.

Most of the time it was the motoring public who wrote the gems of wit. There seemed to be something about seeing those sets of homespun philosophy that made every reader think he or she was a poet laureate.

As a matter of fact, several well known poets earned more than coffee money from knocking out the billboard banter. They never, of course, allowed their names to be exploited along with their petty prose.

Most people, however, tried their hands at the compositions for kicks, not even aware that the company paid up to $100 for accepted jingles. Here are some examples that paid off.

The shaving-cream manufacturers say the most popular Burma Shave rhyme was this one:

Does your husband misbehave,
Grunt and grumble,
Rant and rave?
Then shoot the brute some
Burma Shave.

Some signs were controversial, historic or profound. Others smacked of nationalistic overtones:

We'll shave it yet,
That facial moss,
From that shaggy
Cuban boss.
Burma Shave.

Many motorists will remember chuckling at the thoughts of these limericks:

The beatnik's beard
No more the rave,
They get their kicks from
Burma Shave.

There's a sign
Atop the Kremlin
Placed there by
Our special gremlin.
Burma Shave.

If harmony
Is what you crave
Then get a tuba.
Burma Shave.

Mug and brush
Old Adam had 'em ...
Is your husband
Like Adam, Madam?
Burma Shave.

The bearded lady
Tried a jar
She's now a famous
Movie star.
Burma Shave.

Careless bridegroom,
Dainty bride,
Scratchy whiskers,
Homicide!
Burma Shave.

A peach looks good
With lots of fuzz,
But man's no peach
And never was.
Burma Shave.

Said Juliet
To Romeo,
"If thou won't shave,
Go homeo!"
Burma Shave.

Everyone remembers a couple personal favorites, even the company executives who were queried for this story. A couple of such company classics are:

Riot at drugstore,
Calling all cars,
100 customers,
99 jars!
Burma Shave.

And ...

Don't take a curve
At 60 per,
We hate to lose
A customer.
Burma Shave.

You can see why they like these. The accent on the customer, after all, was the whole idea of the sign campaign.

Each year in January and February, new crops of would-be signs were screened in the jingle contest. In 1938, one of the big years for the company, some 10,000 persons submitted more than 50,000 jingles. These were reviewed and cut to 20, which were ultimately accepted and paid for. Each one the public saw seemed to be classic.

The signs had to be changed annually, like crop rotation, so a message didn't wear out in one spot. So the sign changers could tell which ones had been changed and which ones had not, red ones went up in even years and yellow ones in odd years. These sign changers started in the spring in the northern and eastern parts of the United States, then followed good weather toward the southern and western parts of the country during the fall and winter.

Sites for postings were leased from farmers in exchange for cash each year. This was one crop farmers didn't have to plant, irrigate or cultivate—just harvest!

No accident has ever been caused by motorists reading the signs. Safety first, last and always was another *ipso facto* motto of the company.

Serial signs were used, of course, but with only a very few words painted on each. The signs were then posted a full 100 feet apart, close by the roadside, and only on straight stretches. The serial arrangement actually decreased accidents, since the driver had to travel at a moderate speed to read them— and Mother and the kids always insisted on reading them.

In more recent years, as a matter of fact, a growing number of the jingles have been devoted to highway safety messages. The company felt they were particularly effective since the driver saw them when he was actually behind the wheel of his auto. Also, they were "light" instead of "preachy," so perhaps he would remember them better.

Examples of these are:

Keep well to the right
Of the oncoming car,
Get your close shaves
From the half-pound jar.
Burma Shave.

Past schoolhouses
Take it slow,
Let the little
Shavers grow.
Burma Shave.

If you dislike
Big traffic fines,
Slow down till you
Can read these signs.
Burma Shave.

Famous last words
About lights that shine:
"If he won't dim his,
I won't dim mine."
Burma Shave.

And that is the nutshell history of a national institution, which has gone by the way. About all that can be added is:

We thank you for
The laughs you gave
With roadside ads
Of Burma Shave. ❖

© John Sloane

Grandpa's Flivver

By Albert M. Hall

Back in 1931, when I was 14, I spent the summer with my grandparents in the country. Dad thought it would do me good, but Mom cried a little to see me go. Naturally, anything my parents agreed upon, I disapproved. After all, being a big-city boy, I would be giving up a lot.

My grandparents had a small farm in southern Vermont, near Dorset. There were no horses on the farm, just a couple of cows and a bunch of chickens. It wasn't all that great, and since Grandpa thought he'd broaden my experience by giving me plenty of chores, I worked myself to a frazzle.

As far as I could see, the only interesting thing around the place was Grandpa's old flivver that stood dusty and forlorn in the barn, serving no other purpose than that of a roosting place for the hens. But I suppose Grandpa wanted to bring a little excitement into my life, for he vowed that he would have the car in topnotch condition before the summer was over and would take us into the mountains for a picnic.

I never imagined Grandpa would be able to keep his promise; that old car looked hopeless. Secretly, however, I hoped he would. I was itching to ride in the thing.

With barely a week to go before I returned home to missed friends and city life, I entered the kitchen to the great smell of Grandma's bacon. She seemed happier than usual, humming a tune and fussing over me.

Then I heard it: the sputter and race of a motor. I looked at Grandma. She was smiling.

"He's got it running!" I said, jumping to my feet.

"It sure is running," she said, pulling my ears and rocking my head, "and we're going up in the mountains for that picnic. Your grandfather got the car going yesterday when you were down in the field. You want to go to the mountains today, don't you?"

I nodded and gulped my milk. "Great, oh great! Should I wear my shoes?" By now, I was used to going barefoot.

"You'd better," she said. "We might climb a mountain."

I was out onto the porch in three steps, with one shoe on and the other in my hand. I was trying to run and tie my laces at the same time.

There in the flivver sat Grandpa, a green-and-red hunting cap slung over one eye, and grinning from here to Boston.

I hitched my overall strap over my shoulder, got my shoes tied, and clambered into the front seat next to him. The floorboards shook from the motor as I yelled for Grandma to hurry. She was already running from the house, carrying a large picnic basket, her big floppy farm hat just about ready to fall from her head.

The flivver was calming down to a steady mutter as Grandpa nursed it out of the farmyard and onto the dirt road. "Come on," he said. "Let's see what this Lizzie will do!" His fingers pulled down on the gas lever, and the motor roared.

Looking back, the wind tearing at my eyes, I saw Grandma holding onto her hat. The flivver bucked and bounced and the picnic basket fell from Grandma's lap. Turning around, I saw blue sparks leaping from the magneto box and heard Grandpa give a whoop. I hung onto the side and leaned out, letting the wind whip me. I tried to count the fence posts going by, but couldn't keep up.

The road roughened and we slowed down. "Good gracious," Grandma said. "We want to get to the mountains, not wind up in the ditch."

"How fast we going, Grandpa?"

"'Bout 40 or so. If we went any faster you'd have hollered."

"No, I wouldn't," I said, thinking that it must have been more than 40.

"Don't do it again," said Grandma from the back. Grandpa chuckled and nudged me with his elbow.

We passed a farm and I waved to a girl about my age who was sitting on a horse. I felt pretty good, bouncing along in the flivver, especially with a cowboy like Grandpa at the wheel.

The mountains were plainer now in the south. I could see dark valleys cutting into the slopes and there was a mist on the upper peaks. "We'll be there soon," said Grandpa, glancing down at me.

I guess it must have been midmorning when we left the graded road and chugged up a winding trail with rocks sticking out of the ruts. Ahead of us, the mountains looked low and treeless. They didn't look like mountains at all. I stood up and looked ahead while Grandpa's foot went down on the low pedal and the flivver growled at the grade.

"Come on, Lizzie," said Grandpa, hitching himself back and forward in the seat, as though to help the car over the hill. Then, as we pulled over the hump, there were the real mountains, high into the clouds, emerald green with trees. I looked back at Grandma and she nodded and smiled her appreciation, sitting on the edge of her seat.

I kept standing as the ancient car made the slope. The road got rougher and Grandma called for me to sit down. Grandpa was in a good mood, saying funny things to the car, coaxing it over steep pitches. He talked to it like a horse, patting it on the dashboard, promising it an apple when we got there.

As the trail got steeper, a jet of steam burst from the radiator cap. The car throbbed and labored and we all sat forward, urging it on, but it slowed, shook, stopped and stood there, steaming and shaking as the motor died with a last lunging gasp.

The thought that we had broken down here, on the threshold of our mountain adventure, made me panicky. We were in a bare, rocky gorge. There were few trees, and to the left a stream tumbled down a bouldered channel, but to get to the real mountains, we had much farther to go.

Grandpa grunted and reached over the back-seat for a pail that lay a Grandma's feet. "Can you get down to that creek," he said to me," and bring back some water?"

"Sure," I replied, grabbing the bucket. When I came stumbling back, staggering with the weight of the pail with the water slopping over my shoes, Grandma had already climbed out and was putting a rock under the back wheel.

With his big polka-dot handkerchief, Grandpa made quick stabbing turns at the radiator cap. When the cap finally blew off and steam erupted upward for 6 feet, we all jumped back. In a minute, Grandpa had some water in, but it bubbled back. He poured some more and back it came. Finally, he got it filled. "You two stay here," he said. "Let's see if she'll go over with less of a load."

But the flivver wouldn't. She moved two feet, strangled and died. Grandpa looked at us. We must have looked pretty glum. He winked at me and said to Grandma, "Can you kick that rock from under the wheel?"

"Yes," she said, "but do you think … maybe we could walk from here?"

"Heck with that," said Grandpa. "I'll get her up if I have to carry her on my back."

Grandma kicked the stone away and the flivver rolled backward down the hill, Grandpa craning, steering with one hand. At the bottom he angled the wheels, got out and cranked the motor. It chugged to life and Grandpa was at the wheel again. Then he turned the car around and came up the hill backwards.

The motor roared like a tractor and gravel flew from under the back wheels. The car went past us and up to the crest, where it turned and waited for us to scramble up the hill and jump in.

"Well," said Grandma in relief, "who'd have thought of going up backwards?"

"Got more power in reverse," Grandpa said. "Can't make it one way, try another."

I cheered and stood up again. We were climbing into the mountains.

"How do you like it?" Grandma shouted. I turned and nodded, and she smiled at me. She looked excited; her face was flushed, and the floppy hat falling to one side gave her a reckless, girlish look.

"Hi there, Grandma," I said grinning at her.

"Hi there, yourself," she said, grinning back.

"We're high all right!" shouted Grandpa, and we all laughed and yelled happily.

Needless to say, that one day with the flivver and the picnic that followed made that summer of 1931 a memorable one for me. Unfortunately, it was never repeated, but I'll never forget that afternoon and Grandpa's flivver. ❖

Mongolian War Wagons

By Myrele Dee Cameron

The automobile, like good champagne, improves by stages, or by degrees. But my story is not to discuss the monstrous automobile as we know it today, but the way of life when you owned a car in the Good Old Days.

The automatic starter was not standard equipment in cars for many years. Neither was the gearshift, speedometer, water pressure or gas gauge. Few drivers bothered to obtain a driver's license, insurance or car tags. Probably such things were mandatory, but there were so few cars on the road and even fewer patrolmen to enforce the laws. Speeding certainly was no problem; neither the car's mechanism nor the road surface would permit it. State revenues on cars were too meager to be of much interest to the bureaucracy, which left car owners pretty much to themselves.

I didn't know much about cars, even though I learned to drive a Ford Model T coupe before I was 16. My boyfriend bought a second-hand Model T. As I was his favorite girlfriend, he insisted on teaching me to drive, even though few women drove cars then.

That automobile was as clumsy and hard to manipulate as a Mongolian war wagon, certainly nothing a lady cared to wrangle with. But I suppose I didn't consider myself a lady.

John and I drove outside the city limits, and there, in an Ohio cow pasture, I learned to drive my first car. I was so proud of my achievement and my boyfriend that I married the guy a few years later. I think my girlfriends at old Hamilton High were a little bit jealous of me when they saw me driving a car. The suave electric Broughams were designed with women in mind. They were a short-lived model, however; their driving performance restricted them to paved streets and only the rich could afford them. It was around 1914 when installment financing began to become common, and buying a car was like buying a sewing machine. Still, financing anything was not a popular thing to do back then; going into debt for such unreliable luxury was an automobile was the height of impracticality, many thought, although it was more widely embraced by the young and adventurous.

Will Rogers once said, "There ought to be a law to force all cars off the road until they are fully paid for. It would greatly relieve the traffic congestion." If Will could travel along our six-lane freeways today!

Gasoline stations were widely scattered back then, not blooming on every block and at every crossroad as they do today. And few carried tires or chains. Motorists carried much of their own fuel, oil and spare tires. In fact, service stations did not exist as such; gasoline and oil were bought at general stores or at the few existing garages. Farmers who used gasoline motors to cut wood and pump water usually kept a surplus and advertised on sides of barns or roadside posters if they had gasoline for sale.

For cold weather, there was a detachable roof, a window-like square tent. The sales pitch claimed, "Now you can drive all winter!" Automobiles were usually jacked up in garages or stored during winter months in cold climates, reminding the modern motorist what fair-weather friends the early cars were.

Hudson Motors made the first car with a roof permanently joined to the body, as a coupe and a roadster. Hudson was also the first to make sedans. They only cost $100 more than the touring car; when driving, you wore duster coats, veils and goggles, and still suffered windburn. Those cars had acetylene headlights.

As far back as I remember, in 1912, my Uncle Jim bought the franchise to become the first Ford dealer in our small Kentucky town. Not long thereafter, a man by the name of Hackney bought the franchise to sell Hupmobiles right across the street. 'Twas then the

battle of the brag began as to which car bested the other in endurance, speed, mechanical breakdowns and repair. The old Hup has long since vanished from the highways, but the Ford still hangs in there.

I can see Aunt Jane now, sitting so proudly beside Uncle Jim, her straw hat swathed over and tied under her chin with pink chiffon scarves, her buxom figure securely buttoned from top to bottom in her long, tan dust coat.

Uncle Jim wore gloves, goggles and a billed cap to match his tan dust coat and talked incessantly about the pride of owning and selling Fords. The struggling motor chugging along the rutted roads drowned him out for the most part, but that never discouraged

John and I drove outside the city limits, and there, in an Ohio cow pasture, I learned to drive my first car. I was so proud of my achievement and my boyfriend that I married the guy a few years later.

him from boasting about the touring car's mileage, power and performance.

We kids sat proudly in the backseat, taking in the country sights and laughing at the frightened horses along the way. We were glad to be in the car and not in the surrey or buggy with the other travelers who were also out to enjoy a Sunday drive.

Automobiles in the Good Old Days were never referred to as "cars." They were advertised as "autos" or, colloquially, as "machines," "Tin Lizzies" (Fords), "flivvers," "puddle stickers," "puddle jumpers," "gasoline buggies" and "horseless carriages." Sometimes, when broken down on the road or stuck in a mud hole, they were called names that are unprintable.

Back then, drivers were self-taught, heeding instructions like these from a driver's manual that was printed around 1910–1912:

"When approaching a hill, it is often well to rush it if the coast is clear. The horn or the gong should be used freely, although in blasts of short durations. Don't argue with the trolley car, express wagons, brewery trucks or other heavy bodies found on the public thoroughfares. Remember the drivers … operate on the theory

'Might is right.' The automobile's reputation being in many places none of the best, it is most important to drive as unoffensively as possible. Though it may be distinctly humorous to see an elderly person dancing a fandango in front of a car, such which has caused much needless irritation and dislike for the automobile in general.

"Do not discommode users of the road or inhabitants or roadside houses by raising an excessive amount of dust. Highway driving is in no way related to intelligence, but common courtesy will distinguish you from a careless lout. Don't expect women and children to get out of the way; don't sneak away if you have an accident. Drivers should have a mental test before being allowed to drive. Don't bespatter mud on pedestrians. The art of taking corners without endangering oneself and other road users is worth cultivating 'Drive as if the other fellow hates you and is out to kill you' is some drivers' motto but not a wise one to practice."

In 1914, there were approximately 100 or fewer automobiles per 1,000 population, according to an estimate taken more or less east of the Mississippi River. In 1914, America had only 750 miles of concrete highway. Rains turned other roads into slithering swamps, especially where the underlying soil was clay; in dry weather, the traction was better but the dust was suffocating. And getting lost was inevitable.

The Lincoln Highway was planned as America's first coast-to-coast highway, but west of the Mississippi, it was a hit-or-miss series of dotted patches on the road map along rutted quagmires that would discourage the most adventurous jeep driver. The successful motorists made it only by using towropes and fence-rail levers to get themselves out of sticky situations. Some carried pennants bearing names of their hometowns and left them by the worst places to warn other motorists.

Emily Post, her sister and nephew were among the first travelers to successfully cross the continent by car. That was in 1915, to attend the California-Panama Exposition. The speed limit was 20 mph, and even traveling mostly in low gear, they barely made it through via Raton Pass and Albuquerque. Bridges were scarce. The Automobile Association kept teams of horses in a livery stable to insure that motorists could get through. Even so, it took four weeks. Rainstorms held them up once for many hours, until horse-drawn scrapers smoothed the worst ruts and turned the mud into a tedious but navigable surface.

Still, Mrs. Post and her entourage took great pleasure in pioneering the trip, "… seeing our country for the first time. … Trains only give outskirts of towns," she wrote. "The automobile drove through them."

Ransom E. Olds, who gave his name to the Oldsmobile, boasted that what he was tinkering with would be "far better than the horse. It would never kick or bite; never tire on long runs, nor sweat in hot weather. Does not require stable care and only eats when on the road."

By now the electric trolley had already retired the horses that had once plodded between the horsecar tracks. Gasoline-powered taxicabs were also replacing the hackney cabs—the "hacks"— just as gasoline was rapidly replacing the haystack as the energy source of choice. And sanitation in the city was much improved once the animal waste was absent from streets and livery stables.

Strange as this may sound today, the automobile also meant safer transportation. At that time, the number of motor fatalities was less than a tenth the number of deaths caused by kicking, bucking or runaway horses. My grandfather-in-law was killed while training a horse, and a newlywed great-aunt was killed on her honeymoon, along with her husband, by a runaway buggy.

It was 1916 before the first federal subsidy was granted to improve highways. The internal-combustion engine, V-8 motors and all the electrical gadgets and other improvements in automobiles encouraged the construction of better roads.

And thus the contraption once deemed to be a fad, a rich man's toy and a fool's dream grew into a giant that revolutionized the world, and became a necessity rather than a luxury. It also propelled us along the path toward bigger and greater "contraptions," such as aircraft, spaceships, moon rockets and submarines.

And this was all brought about by a few of great faith in their "Mongolian war wagons" amidst the trepidation of many doubting Thomases, way back in the Good Old Days. ❖

Filler Up! by John Slobodnik, House of White Birches nostalgia archives

The Speedmobile

By Ella Mae Charlton

*I*n the early part of the 20th century, the motor vehicle called "automobile" was coming into prominence. It heralded a breakthrough in transportation that would change lifestyles around the world. But for a child born on a ranch in Childress County, Texas, the sight of such a conveyance back then was rare indeed.

One day, however, a friend of the family invited us to go for a ride in his new Buick. This one ride was enough to give my father "the bug." Only a few days later, he announced his decision to purchase a car. He would ride into Childress with the mail carrier and return the following day with the wonder of wonders.

Before noon of that day, my brother, my sister and I were searching the road as far as our eyes could see—and that was quite a distance, as there was little to obstruct the view. It was not until the middle of the afternoon that we sighted the object we'd been looking for. My brother, six years older than I, shouted with joy and ran down the road to meet it and catch a ride to the house.

From our vantage point on the front porch, we saw the automobile come to a sudden stop only a few hundred feet from the house. We watched while the man who had been driving got out and looked underneath the car. Then he pulled something resembling a long tray from beneath it and tossed it into the ditch.

In a short time he had brought the beautiful gray carriage to a stop right in front of the house. The driver was introduced as Henry Hankins, the Buick dealer in Childress. He had come to stay a few days with us and teach my father to drive.

"Mr. Hankins, what was it that you threw in the ditch?" my mother asked.

"That was the dustpan," he explained. "We hit a high center and I had to take it out so we could move. Besides, that dustpan isn't good for anything; it's only in the way."

Then he suggested we go for a ride and we hastily climbed into the auto. We went on a road through the west pasture that was as good as any road around. After we had gone about half a mile, my brother shouted, "We're making 15 now! Will it go 20?"

"We're going fast enough!" my mother said emphatically. "We'll be lucky if we aren't all killed before we get back home!" She had not been as enthusiastic about this new mode of travel as were the male members of the family. My sister and I were too small to have any opinions.

Early the following morning, the first driving lesson took place in a clearing west of the barn. Mr. Hankins patiently explained in detail the workings of the car to his pupil. My father took the wheel and made the first circle very well but sped up noticeably after that. Around and around

1910 Touring Buick, courtesy TA Performance Products, Inc., Scottsdale, Ariz.

he went, increasing speed with each circle. Mr. Hankins waved his arms and shouted at the top of his voice, but to no avail. My father continued to circle as if he were on a track. It was some time before he managed to bring the car to a stop.

"Mr. Clark," the teacher said, "you were stepping on the gas instead of the brake."

"I don't know what in thunder I stepped on," my father replied, "but you can take this thing back to Childress! I can see that a horse is the only thing I can get along with."

My brother was 12 years old and small for his age but he knew that he could learn to drive. Mr. Hankins was sure that he could, too, and together they persuaded my father to keep the car. The young driver was an apt student, and from then on he was the family chauffeur.

He could hardly wait for Saturday so he could drive us the 10 miles to Hollis, Okla., where we did most of our "trading." As we zoomed along, the driver of every buggy and wagon we met pulled his team as far to the side of the road as he could, then jumped out and held his horses until the motor could no longer be heard. One man shook his fist at us and others shouted something, which—fortunately—could not be understood.

Soon after that we heard reports from friends that it was being rumored that my brother was so short that he had to stand to drive. But the truth was that large blocks had been wired onto the clutch and brake so that he could reach them.

After another trip to town when hostility toward our horseless carriage was evident, my mother approached Papa as he was reading the daily edition of the *Fort Worth Star-Telegram*. "You know," she said, "I think we'd better sell that contraption before some person gets mad enough to kill us."

My father smiled and handed her a section of the paper. "Read this," he said.

"Good glory!" Mama exclaimed after she had read the article. "I know now we'd better get rid of that thing."

The story about a group of farmers in the Midwest who had formed the Farmer's Anti-Automobile League. They had been so incensed when a farm woman had been injured by a car that they armed themselves with pitch-forks and hid along the roadside. When an automobile appeared, they halted it, flourished

their pitchforks under the driver's nose and pushed his car off the road.

"But, Papa, what will we do if they get pitchforks after us?" Mama sounded as if she knew it would happen.

But Papa did not seem the least bit worried. "We'll sound that squawk they call a horn and scare them off."

The "squawk" to which he referred was like a small balloon of black rubber that was squeezed to produce a noise. It was attached to the driver's side of the car, and compared to horns on cars today it made a feeble sound. Before our automobile was a year old, the rubber had gone limp and the horn was gone.

It took a small excuse—or none at all— for the family chauffeur to want to back the Buick out of the shed (we had not heard of "garages") and take a ride. One Sunday afternoon a neighbor girl, Lula, walked the mile and a half to our house. She had never ridden in an automobile, and that was a good reason for us to go for a spin.

We breezed along at 15–20 miles an hour without incident until my mother said it was time we started for home. But the roads were not made for U-turns. My brother said, "I'll go on to the rock house and turn there." There was one remaining half-dugout in that section, and because the upper part was rock and frame, we always referred to it as "the rock house."

Everything was fine until my brother failed to estimate the distance to the fence that surrounded the house. Despite loud shouts of "Whoa! Whoa!" from the backseat and a sudden application of the brakes, into the fence we went. Fortunately, we did not hit a post, and the car had slowed sufficiently so that little damage was done.

After we were on our way again, my mother said, "It's a good thing that fence was there or you would have knocked the house down. If you don't slow down there is no telling what we will hit before we get home."

A few minutes later we had another calamity. Lula became very ill. Whether it was from fright or motion sickness, we never knew; but needless to say, the rest of our trip was hardly as pleasant as the first part. As my brother worked to clean up our prized possession, he grumbled at us. "If you kids have any other friends who want an

This wonderful photo of a family out for a drive in their Buick Touring car was taken by an unknown Vermont photographer in 1912. The year, 1912 can be read on the automobile's front license plate. The Buick appears to be a Model 35 that had an inoperative driver's door. This was the company's most popular model for that year. Copyright 1998, Heritage Photographs

auto ride, you can find another car *and* another driver!"

Although we seldom had enough rain in Northwest Texas, mud was our great enemy when it came to traveling in the car. Whenever we were away from home and observed a cloud that looked remotely like it might have rain in it, we were quickly rounded up to head for home.

There was one "bog hole" where we invariably met our Waterloo, and it was only a few hundred yards from our house. After my brother had made a desperate effort to drive the car out, my father would walk to the barn, saddle his horse and be back within a few minutes. He tied one end of a rope to the saddle horn and the other to the car. The combination of the driver's foot on the gas pedal and the horse's pull enabled us to make it every time.

Our most harrowing trip came later when we went from the ranch to Quanah, a distance of about 60 miles–a half-day's journey. My father had gone to Kansas City with a shipment of cattle. His brother who lived in Quanah was also away from home, and his wife and their son came to visit us. After a few days, the decision was made that Mama, my sister, brother and I would return with them. We took our own car so we would have transportation home. That was the longest trip we ever made in our automobile.

My cousin drove their Cadillac and we followed

close behind in our "speedster." Our young chauffeur was determined that no car, not even a Cadillac, would outrun him. Mama and my aunt wore linen dusters and tied large veils over their hats and faces, securing them under their chins with ribbons. My sister and I, however, had no such equipment, and we literally ate dust for the entire trip. My brother would not have considered dropping far enough behind to avoid the powdery particles.

Besides the endless dust, we also bounced around, sometimes on the floor, sometimes bumping each other as we went flying toward the top of the car.

It was time for the noon meal when we reached Quanah. "You couldn't outrun us, could you?" my brother asked the very first thing.

"I wasn't half trying," Cousin replied tartly. "I was leading the way; I didn't want you to get lost."

Both the old gray Buick and the rock house have passed into history. That Buick, with its side curtains, its squawk, and its 4-cylinder beat, was replaced by many newer models through the years. The rock house stood until a few years ago, when someone removed the frame part, including the supporting beams. Where once a landmark stood, now only a pile of rock and rubble remains.

Unlike the Buick, the old prairie home cannot be improved upon, and it can never be rebuilt as the pioneer homestead it once was. ❖

EIGHT STRAIGHT REASONS FOR A
Straight Eight!

BUICK VALVE-IN-HEAD EIGHT
SILENT OIL CUSHIONED

Buick cars have the genuine economy of all fine and durable things—economy based on quality insured by General Motors science and Buick workmanship

YOU'VE GOT WHAT IT TAKES!

You can afford the new Buick. It's easy to buy and thrifty to own. With all its quality, its phenomenal performance and stunning style, prices start as low as . . . **$765** *and up, list at Flint*

Safety glass standard, accessories slightly extra. Prices subject to change without notice

GENERAL MOTORS TERMS TO SUIT YOUR LIKING

WHEN BETTER AUTOMOBILES ARE BUILT BUICK WILL BUILD THEM

EVERY Buick motor car for 1937 registers striking and substantial style and engineering advances over the best we have previously produced.

Yet the heart of this marvelously good automobile—the quiet, rugged, durable power-plant—remains in its essentials unchanged.

That means the brilliant new Buick, higher-powered in every size and type, has a straight-eight engine— more important than that, *a valve-in-head* straight-eight.

It would have been cheaper for us to have gone to another type engine, or to fewer cylinders, if cost were our chief concern —but we did not, for these eight *straight reasons that ought to appeal to any sensible man's money:*

1. The valve-in-head engine gives ten per cent more power from every gallon of fuel than any other type of engine size for size

2. In the valve-in-head straight-eight you use less fuel per cylinder

3. You have a cleaner running, freer breathing engine

4. You get a smoother flow of power

5. You have less vibration

6. You put less load on the bearings

7. You get longer life from the whole power plant

8. And in the valve-in-head design you have the engineering principle used by every world's record holder on land, water, or in the air

"It's Buick again!"

YOUR MONEY GOES FARTHER IN A GENERAL MOTORS CAR

A Change for the Better

By Elizabeth R. Sphas

A new 1922 Studebaker touring car changed our family's lifestyle. The Sunday stroll or Sunday nap became the Sunday drive. I didn't resist going on those drives the way today's teenagers resist doing things with their parents. I didn't resist anything that meant going somewhere—*anywhere*. My parents said I had an "itchy foot." It wasn't a complaint, just a statement of fact. They knew I got it honestly.

My father was a station agent for the Pennsylvania Railroad so we had passes to ride the trains. We went to Pittsburgh, 21 miles from home, to shop and attend movies. Our town was so small that we could walk everywhere in it. Our auto, as it was called then, was reserved for Sunday drives. Washing it every Saturday was routine.

The pleasure of the Sunday drive was in going, not arriving. We explored every road and country lane for miles around. Often when we came to a crossroad, Father would ask, "Left or right?" Then he'd drive in the direction suggested. I don't remember that we ever became lost. If we did, it didn't matter. Sooner or later we came to a place we recognized. I probably recognized more roads than my parents did. There wasn't much for teenagers to do on dates except "ride around."

Neither do I remember using maps. We had a big atlas, but we didn't use the atlas for our Sunday drives until one day we came to a town named Pancake, named for an early settler. I then studied the atlas and found towns named Brave, Jolly Dime, Eighty-Four, Ten Mile, Amity, Prosperity and Glyde, all in our area. We decided to drive to each one to see what towns with such unusual names were like. This gave purpose to our Sunday drives.

Pig Ear was a mining town about a mile from ours. I've asked dozens of people how it was named, but none knew; perhaps from a miner's expression, "In a pig's ear," a popular slang phrase at that time.

Father drove slowly enough for us to observe; we saw lush flower and vegetable gardens, apple and pear trees in bloom, and dainty spiderwebs glistening in the sun. We picked wildflowers and fallen apples along the roadside. We picked elderberries and blackberries from bushes that lined the back roads for miles. We could often reach the blackberries without even getting out of the auto. We'd return to those bushes on a weekday, properly dressed in old clothes, with long black stockings on our arms to protect them from briar scratches.

We always wore our "Sunday go-to-meeting clothes" on Sunday drives. Everyone, including children, dressed up on Sundays and holidays and stayed that way all day. Many wore "dusters," raincoat-style cover-ups that kept the clouds of dust that blew into the open autos from ruining their good clothes. It would have been more sensible to wear everyday clothes, but that wasn't done in those days. We drove on back roads to avoid the dust raised by heavy traffic on the main roads, as well as to see the soft greens of spring, the vivid colors of autumn.

The front doors of our Studebaker opened from the front, and had extra latches that held the doors open 2 inches to let in more air. It also let in extra dust. Deciding between dust and air was a no-win decision.

We were a picnicking family so we often took along chicken, ham or cold beef left from Sunday dinner, plus pickled eggs, bread-and-butter pickles, cookies and fruit. We ate in the auto unless we could find a clean table and benches in a picnic grove or churchyard.

While eating, we enjoyed watching striped chipmunks fold maple leaves into tiny squares and tuck them into their jaws to hide under tree roots for their winter beds. We chuckled over the antics of young colts, calves and rabbits in the fields. We sometimes stopped to watch dogs round up cows for their evening milking.

All autos had manual gearshifts back then.

After watching Father, I was sure I could drive. The time came when I was old enough to get my license and Father let me practice one Saturday. Our house was at the top of a slope so the auto would start to roll when it wasn't in gear. I got so excited that I let the auto move too fast so the gears grumbled.

Father said I couldn't get my license unless I could shift silently.

Oh, how I tried and tried! But the harder I tried, the louder the gears grumbled. Eventually, however, I mastered them.

After that, *I* was the driver on our Sunday drives. ❖

1935 Studebaker ad, House of White Birches nostalgia archives

© *Sunday Drive* by John Sloane

Are We There Yet?

Chapter Four

Being farm kids who really had never been anywhere in our lives, I promised Janice that if she would marry me, I would show her the world. I decided to start with our honeymoon, so, instead of going somewhere for a few days and then coming back home, we decided we would take two weeks and just drive.

After cutting across country roads through the Boston Mountains of Arkansas, we headed west through Oklahoma and across the panhandle of Texas. We stayed in tourist courts the first couple of nights, but discovered quickly that money would run out long before the trip did at that rate. From then on we slept beside or in our trusty old Ford.

It was slow going across New Mexico and hot through much of Arizona. We drove by night across the desert of western Arizona to Barstow, Calif., to give our oft-boiling radiator a bit of a rest.

"Are we there yet?" is the traditional query of weary travelers. We were lucky. We didn't have children to pester us with that question, we were having too much fun on our first real adventure, and, frankly, we didn't know where "there" was. We were just determined to keep going until we found ourselves "there."

I suppose it was providential that the end of our honeymoon trek was the Pacific Ocean. It was the first time for either of us to see the ocean and we were awed by its grandeur. Sadly, we also realized we had reached "there." If all went right, we would make it back to home and jobs before both time and money ran out.

Altogether we drove over 3,600 miles across nine states on our grand adventure. By not having a real agenda, we found ourselves with plenty of time to stop and see as much of the country as we could. Whether it was the pastoral beauty of a hilly country scene, or the lights of Albuquerque twinkling like diamonds in the valley below, I found Janice's hand in mine or her head on my shoulder as we shared the time together.

We found driving trips suited us. I never got to show Janice all of the world, but in the decades since we have taken many such forays.

Our children were cursed with parents filled with insatiable wanderlust. I know they enjoyed most of our driving vacations, but after hours of seeing new countryside from the side windows of our car, I'm sure they often wondered if we would ever get "there." Often they asked, "Are we there yet?" I always answered their query the same: "I'm not sure where 'there' is, but I'll know it when I see it." So went those wonderful adventures along the Country Roads of long ago in the Good Old Days.

—Ken Tate

Yellowstone for $24

By Helen Scherger Leichner

What a wonderful trip we had. Who would think today that you could take a two-week trip out West and back for just $24? But that is just what we did back in 1940. I lived in the small southern Minnesota town of Dodge Center and taught in a country school near Hayfield. At the end of each school year, I would plan a trip before I went to Rochester to work for the summer.

This particular year, my sister, Esther Scherger, another teacher, Joyce Miller, and two other friends, Edna Fritz and Lorraine Bartel, and I planned to take a trip to see the Black Hills and Yellowstone Park. We decided to put $30 each into the kitty (a cigar box we kept in the glove compartment) to take care of expenses. I had a 1933 Chevrolet four-door sedan, but it had no trunk, so we took out the backseat and put our suitcases down and sat on them.

We drove into Wyoming and got used to the wide-open spaces, often stopping for herds of sheep crossing the highway.

We started out on June 3 at 5 a.m. and drove to Austin to see Joyce's sister, Marjorie Borg, whose husband worked for Hormel's packing plant. From there we drove on to Worthington, where Lorraine stopped to see the Rev. Hetke, a friend of her family. Then we went on to Adrian, where Edna stopped and visited with her uncle for a short time.

Now, with all the family stops out of the way, we went on to South Dakota and stopped in Mitchell for the night. We found a nice tourist cabin for $1.50, and after dinner we drove downtown to see the Corn Palace, a building all decorated with ears of corn. It was quite a sight!

We got up early the next morning, and after breakfast we were on our way again. We drove on through South Dakota until we reached the Badlands National Monument. The roads were terrible and all we could see were rock formations for miles and miles with not a tree in sight.

This photo of Mount Rushmore reveals that the monument had not yet been completed. On the day we arrived, a workman had fallen to his death.

Asking for Directions by Ellen Pyle © 1932 SEPS: Licensed by Curtis Publishing

Left: Potato Creek Johnny pans for gold in the Little Spearfish Creek. He is credited with finding the largest gold nugget in the Black Hills. We enjoyed our chat with him in Deadwood, S.D. Photo courtesy of the Deadwood Chamber of Commerce.

Above: This picture was taken nearly 10 miles from the Devil's Tower in northeastern Wyoming.

We climbed the cliffs and took pictures, but we were glad to leave that area.

Our next stop was Rapid City. Off in the distance, the Black Hills were a beautiful deep purple. We were very excited about seeing Mount Rushmore, as we had read so much about the monument and its great sculptor, John Gutzon Borglum.

At this time, the presidents' faces were still in the making; Theodore Roosevelt's face was just a piece of granite. We arrived at the viewing area to find everything in a state of excitement, with people bustling around. After talking to some people we learned that a worker had fallen to his death that morning. We even got to see Gutzon Borglum at a distance.

After taking pictures of the giant sculpture, we drove south to Wind Cave and Hot Springs. We went down into the cave and watched a man mining for mica. The roads were a sea of ruts, however, and we were glad to get back to the main highway.

We drove into Wyoming and got used to the wide-open spaces, often stopping for herds of sheep crossing the highway. It wasn't long before we reached Greybull, where we stopped to see all that red clay. We were tired by the time we reached Cody and decided to stay there for the night. We found a nice cottage, took showers and then went downtown for dinner. The city was really celebrating, with people milling all around. We soon found out that there was a big dance at the Wolfville Dance Hall.

What a time we had! We were honored guests, and we danced the night away.

The next morning we were on our way again. It wasn't long before we reached Yellowstone Park. We paid our $2 entrance fee and drove toward Yellowstone Lake, where many people were fishing off the long bridge. We went on to the Old Faithful Inn, and we got to see the Old Faithful geyser erupt in all its glory at 4 o'clock sharp. What a beautiful sight to behold!

We rented a cabin for $2 and paid 50 cents for wood. The cabin had a nice stove, so it wasn't long before we had a fired going. After dinner Edna took the leftovers out to the garbage can, but she came running back after being confronted by a bear. She screamed so loud that the bear immediately took off on the run.

We spent the next day looking at all the many geysers and the paint pots with their beautiful colors. The smell of sulfur was everywhere. The wooden walkways with only ropes for handholds were kind of scary, as we thought of what would happen if we fell off.

We drove on to West Yellowstone and Canyon Village, and enjoyed all the beauty of the park. That evening we drove up to Gardenier, Mont., for dinner. It was the first good steak dinner we had had since leaving Minnesota. Then we drove back into the park and stayed at Mammoth Hot Springs. There was so much to see! We were very perturbed, however, at having to pay 39 cents for a gallon of gasoline in the park; elsewhere it was 19–25 cents a gallon.

We rose early the next morning and headed for Mount Washburn; it was one of the highest peaks in the park, and we were anxious to drive to the top. After Tower Junction, our car climbed to an elevation of 10,000 feet, and before we knew it, we were caught in a blinding snowstorm. When I stopped the car to clean the snow off the windshield, I found that my saddle

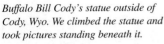

Buffalo Bill Cody's statue outside of Cody, Wyo. We climbed the statue and took pictures standing beneath it.

This is my 1933 Chevrolet sedan that we drove out West. From left to right: Lorraine Bartel, Esther Scherger, Edna Fritz, Joyce Miller and myself, Helen Scherger.

oxfords were no match for the deep snow. It took a long time to cross that peak, as many cars had stalled in the deep snow, but we finally made it down that mountain.

After that ordeal, we decided we had seen all we wanted, and we drove back to Cody. We were glad to be on level terrain again and we enjoyed the warm sun and mild weather.

After a good night's sleep, we started out to see Buffalo Bill's Museum. All those old guns and old clothes from another era were most interesting. We drove out to the Buffalo Bill statue and took pictures. We also saw Buffalo Bill's grandson near some teepees that were on display. We enjoyed talking to him.

We drove on to Moorcraft and decided to see the Devil's Tower, a natural rock formation of volcanic origin resembling a petrified tree stump that rose 800 feet in the air. The top of the tower covers an area of about 1½ acres. We took pictures of this impressive sight, too.

We planned to spend a few days at Lead and Deadwood. We wanted to see all those saloons in Deadwood and see where gold was mined.

The next day we were walking down the streets of Deadwood when we ran into a little old man who told us he was Potato Creek Johnny. He took us to the museum and showed us the biggest gold nugget he had found. We really enjoyed his stories and didn't realize until later that he was such a colorful figure.

We also visited the gravesites of Wild Bill Hickok and Calamity Jane, and in the evening we visited the saloons and dance halls. We were amazed at how much money was gambled at the No. 10 Saloon, where Jack McCall had shot Wild Bill Hickok back on Aug. 2, 1876. We hated to leave Deadwood as it was such a lively place.

Our next stop was Wall, S.D., where we had a Coke at the famous Wall Drug Store. We decided to drive up to Pierre and see what the capitol looked like, and we then drove on to Fort Pierre and found a cabin in a tourist camp. After dinner we went to the theater and saw a double feature, *The Saints Double Trouble* and *Virginia City*.

When we got back to our cabin, Joyce and Edna sat on the bed and it collapsed. Moths and beetles were flying everywhere in the room. All of us said, "Let's get out of here!" We got our belongings together and I got our $1.50 back. We drove back into town, looking for a hotel, but everything was closed. It was 2:30 in the morning.

Filling up the gas tank, we decided to drive on. By now we were all very anxious to get home. We hadn't had any car trouble except for a flat tire back in Cody.

When we finally got home, we had $30 between us, so we each got $6 back. It had only cost us $24 each for that beautiful two-week visit to the Black Hills and Yellowstone Park. ❖

Rambling Along in a Rumble Seat

By Marjorie D. Baechler

When we were small girls, my sister Ginny and I made several memorable summer vacation trips from our home in Connecticut to Grandmother's house in Nova Scotia. Riding in a 1928 Ford rumble seat over 850 miles of roads that were mostly unpaved and surfaced with crushed stone required the stamina of youth and a strong stomach. Hour after hour we huddled together, heads down to avoid the constant wind. Our pilot was Uncle Harold, mother's bachelor brother, who hadn't the faintest notion of the need for frequent rest stops.

Off to New Glasgow, 1934.

Mother, of course, rode in the front seat with 2-year-old Connie beside her. When our need to stop was desperate, we'd beat on the back window for her attention. We quickly learned to time our requests so that we could "hold on" for another 15 minutes at least; Uncle Harold was not about to be ordered to stop until *he* saw fit.

The trips began at dawn on Saturday so we would be well beyond Boston by afternoon. No superhighways wafted us northward—only endless strips of two-lane, winding roads that went around sweeping curves, uphill, down dale, and through each and every city and hamlet. It might have been hard on the driver, but we loved going through the cities and towns. We longed to stop in every one, but we were realistic about Uncle's proclivity for eating and sleeping in remote clusters of cabins set back from the road.

The first night's stop was always the best because we seldom drove beyond the lower reaches of Maine. Route 1 meanders along the coast, and our cabins were often at York Beach or Old Orchard, giving us a chance for a quick, bone-chilling dip in Maine's toe-tingling ocean waters. Early to bed, we were up again at dawn, to ride miles and miles before breakfast. Our empty stomachs sometimes were rebelling by the time we crawled out of our blanket cocoons and literally staggered into the diner.

Our second night on the road was sure to be spent in Grant's Cabins near Ellsworth, Maine. These dinky little predecessors to modern motel units were painted pink and lavender, and scattered in an arc across an unmown field. The amenities included two outhouses but no running water. The food served in the main building was limited to tinned soup, boiled hot dogs and scrambled eggs—when we'd been dreaming all day of a really scrumptious chicken dinner. Oh well, maybe tomorrow. If we did happen to stop in a truly good restaurant, it was a miscalculation on Uncle's part; he seemed to feel his traveling companions were better suited to dingy diners.

Several highlights of our many trips remain in our memories. There was always the thrill of stopping at the Customs House where, after routine questioning, we left our own country at Calais, Maine, and entered Canada at St. Stephen, New Brunswick. We girls secretly anticipated being detained, but it never happened.

Off to New Glascow, 1931.

Once across the border, we perked up and waved to farmers in their fields, counted cows and sheep, and wondered how long it would be until we would see "the map"—a large, beautiful, relief map replica of Nova Scotia, set in a parklike information center that welcomed visitors to the maritime province. We always stopped here! Nova Scotia, after all, had been Mother and Uncle's home for many years.

One fondly remembered stop was an unscheduled night at Pineo Wilson's by the Sea, a magnificent old sea captain's house set on a cove of the Nova Scotia shoreline. That evening, we girls were popped into a hot tub and dressed in our smocked dimity frocks. Supper included fresh Nova Scotia salmon and strawberry shortcake. After this delectable treat, we strolled the beach in the twilight, wishing on the first star that we could stay forever. But Grandmother was waiting.

By noon the very next day, we rolled up Kirk Hill, around the corner past Cantley's brownstone, red-roofed "castle" and into her yard. Yes, the cherry tree was still there— and the big barn—and Uncle Bill's garden. The hammock swung idly between the two tall maples. Cousins clambered over the car, clamoring for our attention. We had arrived! We had nine whole halcyon days to enjoy before we would pile into the rumble seat for the return trip to Connecticut and our waiting Daddy. ❖

Dad's "Campcar"

By Helena Charles Chapman

"Recreational vehicles" were unheard of when my father, Harry Charles of Findlay, Ohio, built the one shown in these pictures. Dad had experience because this was the second one he built. He called his house on wheels a "campcar."

The one shown was built on a 1925 Chevrolet truck chassis. Dad installed all—well, *almost* all—of the comforts of home. He had sleeping arrangements, of course. He had a space heater and a small coal bin.

We made many happy trips with Dad in his "campcar" up to the Toussaint River north of Findlay. Dad loved to fish and my brother, Harold, inherited the same desire. Dad would catch turtles and Mother would have to cook them.

Later, Harold had his own "campcar"—but it was one that he bought and put on the back of a pickup truck. ❖

Harry's "campcar" even boasted a back porch.

Members of the family stand proudly beside the hand-built "campcar."

Hold Your Hat

As told by Albert Tessler to Dick Davis

*I*t was an adventure of dangerous passage, a spectacle of star-clustered skies, a time when migration to California was exciting because the land was still open and handsomely rugged.

In the sweltering heat of September 1923, Albert Tessler, his older brothers Joe and Dave, and mother, Esther, climbed aboard their new Ford Model T touring car, embarking on an arduous 21-day trip from St. Louis to Hollywood. Frank, the eldest brother, went to California after the others.

As the four set off, Esther, a Russian immigrant who had raised the four sons after her husband died, settled into the Ford's backseat. Gingerly she placed beside her the box containing her favorite chapeau. There was no going anywhere in style without it.

Once outside St. Louis, Missouri was largely rural, with axle-rattling dirt lanes that slowed travel. It took the Tesslers five days to leave their home state. Top cruising speed was 35 miles per hour. As for accommodations and conveniences, there were none. The foursome pitched a tent at the end of each day and prepared the evening meal. And Esther made sure her hat was safe.

Gingerly Esther placed beside her the box containing her favorite chapeau. There was no going anywhere in style without it.

Albert, then 21, remembered: "As we approached the Rocky Mountains in Colorado, we had to traverse the torturous Ratoon Pass, with its numerous hairpin curves and perilous sloping roads of mud and rock. We barely made 15 miles per hour.

"To keep from sliding over the mountainside," he continued, "one of us had to hang out on the running board of the car to help counterbalance the sloping road."

After the dangerous course through the mountains, the Ford descended into California, where the Tesslers rejoiced at the paved roads and warm nights. "We slept out of our tents on cots under a most spectacular heavenly display with stars so close, they appeared to touch the earth," Albert recalled.

Their journey continued. Hollywood, a booming town of movie glamour and orange trees, lay just ahead.

The family finally reached their destination at noon one day in late September. They arrived just in time to witness an automobile accident, common even in those early days. During the excitement, Esther sat on the hatbox, crushing her prized chapeau beyond repair and providing a family anecdote that has been told with relish ever since.

The family rented a house for $40 a month. Esther lived a long life and all her sons raised families.

In the years to come, Albert found great satisfaction in having made that extraordinary excursion and then watching California grow for the next 59 years. ❖

To Grandmother's House We Go!

By Mary Foote Marsh

To Carol and Sally—Who Never Experienced the Fun of the Ford

When I was a young girl growing up in Superior, Wis., one of the few things my family did together was to hop—or, I should say, *squeeze*—into the old Ford and ride out to my grandparents' farm in Maple, Wis. There was not much room in the old car with all five of us kids, plus my mother, Aunt Olga and Cousin Betty, so there was a lot of chattering and shifting around before we all got settled and on our way.

Sometimes we would ride only a short distance before Dad would pull over and ask, "Who wants to run along behind the car?" Needless to say, the fear of being left behind quieted us down.

I liked to sit on my brother Milton's knee. His was the least bony of the three older boys, and he never sang in my ear. And how we did sing! My dad, who had a very nice voice, would start us out with his favorite, "I've been working on the railroad, all the live-long day. …" That old song was not far from the truth. Dad had started working for the Soo Line around age 14, when his dad was an engineer, and he was still employed there a year before he died.

After we had sung our way through *The Big Rock Candy Mountain* and *K-K-K-Katy* and *There Was an Old Man Who Had a Wooden Leg*, I'd start staring out the window, wondering if and when we were ever going to get to the old mill. It was the halfway point between home and the farm on Highway 13.

After driving through Sleepy Hollow, a little farm set beside the river, someone would say, "We're coming to the steep climb and the scary turn," and we would all start to tighten our grip on whatever or whoever was handy. After a shift of gears, the Ford would start to climb up the hill. Today, when I travel this road, I can't imagine why we were all so frightened; it really isn't all that high. But back then, we were scared, and my dad made the most of the situation. He got a kick out of pretending to be too close to the edge and watching us cover our eyes and peek through our fingers.

As we neared the curve, he would decide to fill his pipe. As he would reach into his pocket for tobacco and matches, the car would veer a little to one side, and we would scream and ask Mom to fill it. She would take his pipe, fill it and return it to his mouth. I thought she was the cleverest person ever; imagine, a *woman* being able to do that!

As we reached the top of the hill, we would come upon the mill. As many times as we had seen it, it never failed to impress us. Back then it sat in a state of quiet disrepair, not having been used for years. This was the mill to which Grandpa Lammi had brought his wheat to be ground into flour. In those days he would hitch up the old black horse, load up

© *The Gathering* by Bob Pettes

the wagon, drive the 20 miles to the mill, and wait for the wheat to be ground. Then he would load the sacks of flour on the wagon and return over the rough road to the farm. Whenever I ate a slice of Grandma's bread, I couldn't help but think of all the work that went into making it.

After the mill there was not much to see besides barns, cows and farmland, so usually I let the rest of my body join my already-sleeping backside and take a little nap. Waking to the sound of excited voices, I knew that Mom and Aunt Olga were reminiscing about Auntie Skarpakka's old house, which we were passing. This was the house in which their whole family had lived when they first came to Maple. Five people—my grandma and grandpa, my mom, Aunt Ellen and Uncle Toivo—had lived there, crowded in the small attic loft, until Grandpa finished their own house down the road. As I looked across the fields, I could see that three-room house and the old, weathered barn.

To get to the farm we had to go down a steep hill, cross a creek and try to make it up the other side. If the weather was nice, the hill was no problem. But if it had recently rained, we would all have to get out and Grandpa would bring the old black horse to help us up the muddy slope. And if it was wintertime, we would park the car on the hill's crest and plunge our way through the waist-high drifts to the house.

Summertime was the best time to visit because when we came through the gate, Grandma and Musti, the big black sheep dog, would be waiting. After we had hugged Grandma and petted the dog, each of my brothers would take a turn at having Grandma stand under his outstretched arm to see how short she was (under 4 feet, 11 inches). Then my youngest brother and I would run off to see the new kittens in the barn, check the cow pies on our way down to the creek to pick cowslips, peek into the sauna, and look down the well, laughing about the time Grandma's old buckle overshoes had caught together as she was dipping her buckets, and how she had just missed falling in headfirst.

We used to love to open the door of the summer kitchen, where Grandma made butter. Sometimes she would let us take a turn at the churn. Whenever she churned, she would hum some old Finnish song to the accompaniment of the flies' buzzing. To this day, whenever it's warm outside and I hear flies buzzing, I can't help but think of that old outside kitchen.

After picking a big yellow apple from one of the old, gnarled trees that stood by the house, Dick and I would watch the older brothers and Betty playing around on the old farm equipment. Then we'd go into the house to listen to Grandma, Mom and Olga recalling the past.

In 1910 they originally had booked passage on the Titanic, a ship of the Cunard Line. They had been accepted, but later they were told that they would have to take another ship, the Victoria, because the spaces available on the Titanic had been miscounted. Grandpa was already in this country, having come over a few years earlier to work at a lumberyard in Mellen, Wis.

None of them knew a word of English when Grandma and her children sailed from Finland to Liverpool, England, and then to Montreal, Quebec. They traveled by train from Sault Ste. Marie to Superior, Wis., and on to Maple.

They also talked about how hard they had worked at the old Superior Hotel (which burned down in the early 1940s) and how Mom had met my dad there when he was working in the hotel tobacco shop. They talked about all of the famous show-business people Olga had met when she worked as a chambermaid at one of the old hotels in Duluth, Minn. (I still have a beautiful mirror that my aunt received from one old vaudeville performer.) They would laugh together, recalling all the vacations the sisters had given up in order to come home in the summer and help Grandpa and Toivo make hay.

As the shadows started to fall across the old barn, Dad would come in from lying under an old poplar tree and inform us that it was time to head for home. After everyone had made a trip to the outhouse, kissed Grandma and Grandpa, been told for the sixth time that we did not need another cat at home, and petted Musti, Mom and Olga would take their jars of long-milk starter (Finnish yogurt) and we'd all pile back into the Ford. The who's-sitting-where and who's-sitting-on-somebody's-something would start, and a little way down the road, the car would stop, then start again, without anyone running along behind. Grandma would wave us out of sight as we began to see kerosene lamps in farmhouse windows flicker on in the country darkness. ❖

Big Bend Safari

By Dewey Tidwell

rom the time the first Spanish explorers saw what became known as the Big Bend country of Texas, that vast wasteland has been an enigma to man. It was sparsely settled by courageous and hearty ranchers and miners from time to time. Over the years, outlaws and Mexican bandits jostled with the ranchers and miners for supremacy. Finally it was established as a national park by the U.S. government.

I first saw the Big Bend country in 1930, when I was working as a druggist for the Pennington Drug Co. in Alpine. One Sunday morning, R.B. McEntire (of the McEntire Ranch near Sterling City) picked me up bright and early in his Ford Model T roadster. We were headed for El Porvenir, a new hamlet on the Rio Grande, via Valentine, about 75 miles west of Alpine. One of our mutual friends who had been a border patrolman along that stretch of the Rio Grande had homesteaded on 640 acres along the river and had started the settlement of El Porvenir a

The lazy Rio Grande near El Porvenir, Texas.

couple of years earlier. R.B. and I were looking forward to seeing him and his wife again.

The "road" from Valentine to El Porvenir wasn't a road at all. It followed arroyo beds, animal trails and high-peak landmarks all the way to El Porvenir, and when we finally arrived at that remote place, both of us felt like we had been riding a bucking horse. The Model T bounced over rocks, climbed embankments and, in general, rode like a tractor; hence, our jarred feelings.

Our host and his wife were glad to see us, for they seldom saw anyone other than Mexicans who crossed the river to barter sheep, goats, wool and mescal in exchange for the merchandise in our friends' small store. Noting our washed-out appearance, our friend asked us if we would like a drink. The offer of "a drink" in that part of the world always meant an alcoholic drink of some sort, and our friend produced two bottles of liquor—one amber in color and the other a dark brown. When he asked whether we preferred Rio Grande lightning or cactus juice, I chose cactus juice because he said it was milder. But R.B. allowed as how he wanted something with power in it, so he chose the lightning.

After a couple of refills and a short visit, we departed our friends' ocotillo-and-mud home and headed for Shafter, an old, abandoned mining camp, and Terlingua, where quicksilver had been mined for years. Both were about 70 miles away to the southeast.

It was already about 4 o'clock in the afternoon, but the fortification we had received from the "snake medicine" at our friends' home had restored our energy. We felt equal to a couple more hours of jostling before we began hunting for a campsite.

It was about 6 o'clock when we finally began to look for a suitable spot to spend the night. A dry arroyo bed of soft sand beckoned us. After unloading the Model T of cots, blankets, pots, pans and water, I busied myself looking for dead mesquite limbs for a fire while R.B. set up camp. The sun already had gone down. I had collected a sizable armful of limbs, but I decided to add one more to the stack. I stooped to pick up a nice piece that lay at the base of a mesquite tree. But just as I touched the limb, I heard a rattlesnake rattle and the snake lashed out at the limb. I was almost petrified. I still don't know how I did it, but the next thing I remember, I was headed toward camp—sans wood.

R.B. had heard the commotion and met me in midflight. After I told him what happened, both of us went back to the scene, dispatched the snake from some brush near the mesquite tree, gathered up my limbs and made our way back to the camp. Fortunately, our friends at El Porvenir had given us a bottle of Rio Grande lightning to take with us, and we both took a good dose of that "snake medicine" right then and there.

With our nerves soothed by the liquor, we prepared a meal and enjoyed it. Then we turned in quite early so as to get a good night's sleep before the next day's trip. But along about midnight I was awakened by lightning off in the Tierra Vieja Mountains, and in no time flat it began to rain. The rain fell—lots of it—and before we could get the Ford to dry ground, water was running freely in the arroyo bed. That galvanized us into action; we grabbed our camping gear and scrambled to safety. Good thing, too; we had no sooner reached the car when a big wall of water, rocks, limbs and debris flashed right by us. That taught us a lesson about camping in dry arroyo beds. They never are completely safe from flash floods.

The next day, bouncing over rocks and in and out of gullies, we managed to reach Shafter, where we spent the night. One

Our friends' home in El Porvenir.

R.B.'s Ford Model T roadster.

old prospector still lived there and acted as care-taker for a couple of abandoned mines nearby. After a visit with him over frijoles, bacon, coffee and some cookies, we turned in and got a good night's sleep. Early the next morning we were winding our way again over the trackless terrain, heading for Terlingua.

The tall, silver ocotillos swayed in the breeze and reminded us of the story we had heard about a cowboy on one of the area's few ranches. Early one morning, he rode out to check on some cattle. As the sun was coming up in the east, the swaying plants looked like sabers to him as the light hit them. He almost rode a horse to death, riding to Alpine to warn the residents that Mexican bandits were headed that way.

We chose a campsite on high ground late that afternoon. It was in an "orchard" of giant cactus and we thought the setting was most appropriate. Again I set out to get firewood while R.B. set up camp. I had my arms full of dry limbs and was headed back to camp when I heard a roaring noise that reminded me of a swarm of mad yellow jackets I had encountered when I was a kid. By the time I discovered the source of the noise, a swarm of wild bees was on me and my wood. The population in a hive had grown too large, and in their search for a new home, that bunch, with a queen bee in their midst, had chosen me. They literally covered me, though they didn't sting me at first.

I hurried to the camp, bees and all, yelling to R.B. to put coal oil on a stick and have it ready for me when I reached the car. He did just that, and when I reached the car, I jumped into it, bees and all, and grabbed the oil-soaked stick that R.B. had ignited.

"Run like heck away from the car and lie flat on the ground!" I yelled as I began to wave that burning stick in the car. The smoke soon drove

When we finally arrived at El Porvenir, both of us felt like we had been riding a bucking horse. The Model T bounced over rocks, climbed embankments and, in general, rode like a tractor; hence, our jarred feelings.

the bees from the car and they settled on a large cactus a short distance from our campsite. They had found a new home, for the old plant had been punctured many times by peckerwood birds. Again we fled our campsite and finally found another where no signs of bees were evident.

On the third day of our trip we arrived at the old mining camp of Terlingua. Quicksilver was still being mined there by Mexican miners, and they and a few Anglos made up the population of the forsaken-looking place. And it was hot! The heat was intense. It is ironic that a group of men and women calling themselves "chili lovers" gather at that place every year and have a "chili cook-off," choosing a winner for the best concoction. I understand that the beer flows freely, which no doubt helps temper the heat of both nature and the red chili pods. Our coolest drink while in Terlingua was a shot of hot tequila.

Being so near the Santa Elena Canyon of the Rio Grande, R.B. and I drove there to get a view of the breathtaking scenery. Back then, very few Texans ever visited that area.

On our way back to Alpine, R.B. and I camped one night in the area of the Davis Mountains, hoping to catch a glimpse of the famous Ghost Lights. The first report of the lights being seen by a white man was by a Spanish explorer who visited the Big Bend in the 17th century.

When the Alpine and Marfa country began to be settled by cattle and sheep people, the lights were reportedly seen by a number of them. The lights always danced back and forth among the mountain peaks, but no one ever got close enough to determine their origins. Scientists from as far away as Europe visited the area and tried to solve the mystery, but to this day, the Ghost Lights of the Davis Mountains remain as mysterious as ever. ❖

Summer Vacation

By Richard Taylor as told to Marie Melody Taylor

Modern families traveling from one motel to the next probably do not experience the same thrill and anticipation that we used to feel on our summer trips to the cottage when we were young.

When we saw Dad go out in the back yard with a hammer and saw, we all knew what he was doing. It was almost time for our summer vacation to Bush Lake. That hammering and sawing was music to our ears.

But Mother would sigh and say, "What a racket!" The trip meant a lot of work for her, washing and packing and assembling the odd paraphernalia we would need.

In just a few hours, Dad could transform a handful of pine boards into a fantastic 12-foot rowboat. Each year the boat was the same: flat on the bottom and made with tongue-and-groove boards. We watched as he caulked the joints and filled the boat with water so the joints would swell. He did this to make sure that the boat wouldn't leak when it was put into the water.

I remember Dad saying, "OK, boys, let's all go to the hardware for the oarlocks." And after that, we had to go to Sears, Roebuck to buy just the right pair of oars. What fun! If Dad was in a particularly happy mood, he would say, "Bet you fellas could go for a cone." That meant that on the way back, we would stop at our favorite ice-cream parlor. Dad's patience grew thin, for it was difficult for us to choose the flavor we wanted. After we finally had finished, Dad would say, "Back to work."

When we got home, he painted the boat and printed the name "Battleaxe" on the side as a joke to tease Mother. Year after year he would build a new boat, and each one would be named Battleaxe, then Battleaxe 1, 2 and so forth. It was quite a sight to see all those boats named Battleaxe floating around on the lake, with consecutive numbers on their sides.

But there was still one more thing the boat needed. Dad would send us all scurrying for an old can to make an anchor. He filled the can with concrete and attached rings to hold the ropes.

If we were going during the early part of the summer, Dad would tell my brothers and me to collect night crawlers and worms so that we would be ready to go fishing. Sometimes it was late in the summer, and then we would go cricket hunting. But first we had to build a box for the crickets. It would be about 2 feet square with a screen tacked across the front. Then my brothers and I ran all over the neighborhood, looking for crickets under old billboard papers and trash that was lying in the streets. It was a lot of fun to see who could find the most crickets. We put chunks of muskmelon rind in the box to feed the crickets so they would still be alive when we arrived at the cottage.

Finally everything was ready. Mother would call my two oldest brothers to pack the pickup with groceries and put the Battleaxe on top. Dad put the old cane poles on top of the family Pontiac and strapped the suitcases to the running boards and the luggage rack on the back. We all piled in and Dad would say, "Let's go!" Our trip of 150 miles was ready to begin.

After traveling for what seemed like days, we would arrive at the cottage, hot, tired and hungry. The cottage we stayed at was called "the annex" because it was located around from the main house where Aunt Cindy lived. Six rather primitive cottages nestled around hers, and they were inhabited by various relatives throughout the summer. They all had run-down outhouses out back that housed the local spiders and the latest Sears, Roebuck catalog.

Aunt Cindy was a lovable woman who hadn't changed much since the turn of the century, when she had purchased hundreds of acres of property for 25 cents an acre. She hugged us all and spent most of her time

The vacation was now over. We were all a little sad, but as we pulled into our own yard with the turtles, neighbors came from all over to see what we had caught.

waiting on us. She typified the old-fashioned mother with her long, black skirt and her waist-length hair pulled up in a knot on the back of her neck where it was held with a large comb. Her home was the center of activity as we all swarmed in and out through her creaky screen door from dawn until dusk.

We could hardly wait to head down to the lake's edge to launch the newest Battleaxe. Sure enough, there, floating on the lake, were all the previous Battleaxes.

We had waited all year to fish, but we would find that with so many of us enjoying it, we would soon have a shortage of bait. My brothers and I would scout around old abandoned farms that dotted the landscape during those Depression years. Under old manure piles we found plenty of red worms and we hurried back to the boat with them.

One old farm that we really enjoyed visiting was owned by a friendly couple who supplied milk to all the vacationers. Early every morning you could hear the wife chugging along the dirt road in an old 1925 Buick coupe, with the milk bottles rattling in the back. They had a white sway-backed horse that wandered all over, as there were no fences to keep it confined. We looked forward every summer to taking turns riding it.

Poor Mother! It wasn't much of a vacation for her. She spent most of her time preparing food for the next meal. She cooked on the old two-burner kerosene stove, and it required a lot of patience just to light the burners. And whenever she needed water, she had to stand on a box and vigorously work the handle of the pump that was housed in a shedlike room at the back of the cottage.

When we first arrived, before Mother could even put the perishables in the old wooden ice-box, Dad had to drive around the lake and buy ice by the pound. "Clint," she would say, "you better go after the ice." There was an icehouse on the lake where ice that had been cut the previous winter was stored in sawdust.

Dad would say, "Give me about 25 pounds," and the man would place the chunk of ice on the car bumper with a pair of ice tongs. From there, the ice dripped a path back to the cottage.

Often Dad would take us all into the nearby town of Prescott. After bounding along on the dusty, bumpy roads for 7 miles, we were ready for the sodas at the little drugstore. Our yelling and bouncing up and down on the old metal stools must have been frustrating to the heavy man in the long white apron behind the counter.

He would wipe his brow with the dirty apron while we kept changing our minds on the flavor of soda we wanted. Huffing and puffing, he lumbered up and down, impatiently saying, "Make up your mind, kids. I haven't got all day."

Finally we were all satisfied and drove contentedly back to the cottage.

Shortly before our vacation was over, Dad would say, "OK, boys, it's time to catch the turtles." We always took about 30 feet of copper wire line with a heavy hook at one end that we baited with a 1-inch chunk of beef. After driving a spike into a log on shore and securing the other end of the line around it, we cast the hook out into deep water. We were trying to catch snapping turtles, and they were night feeders.

In the morning when we checked the line, we might find a turtle that weighed 25–30 pounds. As they were caught, they were kept in 55-gallon oil drums. When we had caught six or so, Dad would tell us that was enough. The day that we were ready to leave, the turtles were removed from the drums and put in boxes for the trip home.

The vacation was now over. We were all a little sad, but as we pulled into our own yard with the turtles, neighbors came from all over to see what we had caught. There was always a lot of joking and teasing because they all knew what was gong to happen.

Mother would say, "Clint, get the soup cauldron out while I am cutting up the turtles." Well, Dad would get busy in the back yard, starting a fire and filling the cauldron with water. Then our relatives and neighbors were all invited to a turtle feast. The awful odor of the cooking turtles permeated the neighborhood. But none of us seemed to care much, as it was a good reason to all get together again and reminisce about the wonderful summer we had had on our yearly sojourn to the cottage. ❖

Old-Time Vacations

By Marjorie Covalt Yokaitis

*D*espite today's violent world, people once again are opening their doors to vacationing families seeking overnight lodgings for bed and breakfast. Back years ago, that's what a good many people did. Many people seeking to increase their incomes opened up their homes, calling them "tourist homes." They advertised by putting a sign on their front lawn: "Tourist Home" or perhaps "Overnight Guests."

In the mid-1930s, Mom and Dad were in a financial position to travel. Their three oldest children had left home and only I remained, so I was always included in their two-week vacation plans. Dad worked at Ball Brothers Co. where the famous Ball jars were made. Since many women canned to keep food on the table, Ball Brothers was booming.

In one tourist home, I went to the bathroom to take a bath. I had just gotten out of the tub and was drying myself when a man popped in the door. His face turned red with embarrassment and mine did, too.

Our trips took a good deal of planning and preparation. Mother washed and ironed two weeks' worth of clothes, and since there was no such thing as a laundromat, we took along a large denim bag to hold the dirty laundry.

Mother also packed such items as Italian Balm (a fragrant hand lotion), Pond's face cream and powder, Tangee lipstick and metal hair rollers. In those days, the fashionable hairdo consisted of a smooth crown surrounded by little sausage curls. About every third night it was necessary to put up one's hair on the metal curlers. How we managed a good night's sleep in those uncomfortable curlers I will never know.

Also included in our suitcases was a first-aid kit, which contained gauze, adhesive tape, aspirin and a box of baking soda in case Dad got an upset stomach. Mercurochrome and Unguentine were also among the first-aid articles included. Mother apparently was not yet sold on Kleenex, although they were on the market by 1929, so she packed plenty of colorful, frilly handkerchiefs. She did use the familiar pop-up box of Kleenex for cleaning off her cold cream, though.

When the big day arrived, we would get up early—sometimes as early as 4 a.m. We'd eat breakfast somewhere along the way. We would enjoy the beautiful changing scenery, and when I became restless, we would play games, such as how many white houses I could see or how many red barns I could spot. Sometimes we would just sing a favorite tune.

At about 4 o'clock in the afternoon we would begin looking for a likely place to stay overnight. The criteria for a good home included a well-trimmed lawn, sparkling windows and a well-painted exterior. By such evidence of good housekeeping, we could be assured of a comfortable, clean room. We would pull into the driveway and Dad would go in to have a look-see while Mother and I remained in the car. We were always happy when he came out smiling and said, "It's OK."

Usually it was a big, two-story home with many bedrooms. After we had climbed the stairs, Mother and I would take off our dresses and lie down for a nap before dinner.

Dad, always the gregarious soul, would go downstairs to become better acquainted with our hosts. He had a magnetic personality and he truly loved people. Within a half-hour, he would convince our hosts that they were the finest people that walked the earth. As a result, we received the red-carpet treatment. And when it was time to leave, you would have thought we were long-lost relatives. They carried our bags downstairs for us and hung onto the car, talking to Dad until Mother and I wondered if we would ever get back on the road.

We nearly always were able to find a lovely room, but I remember one time when we didn't. We were in the South traveling on a treacherous mountain road. It was hazardous enough already, but when it began to rain, it was impossible. Mother said, "Let's take the first tourist room we find," and we did! It was the most horrible room I had ever seen. Splotched brownish wallpaper hung from the ceiling and walls, and the bathroom was just a hole in the wall. Mother made the mistake of saying, "I'll bet we find bedbugs here." That's all it took for me; I felt bedbugs crawling up and down my legs all night long. We never did find one, but to me, they were there!

On one trip to Florida, we got a nice room and then went driving around, looking for a restaurant. An enterprising newsboy, spying our Indiana license plate, shouted, "Snow in Indiana!" We bought a paper immediately because it was October, and snow in that month was rare indeed. When we found absolutely nothing about snow in Indiana in that newspaper, we had to laugh at our gullibility.

In one tourist home, I went to the bathroom to take a bath. I had just gotten out of the tub and was drying myself when a man popped in the door. His face turned red with embarrassment and mine did, too. He quickly shut the door and hurried down the hall.

After I was dressed, I went back to our room and laughingly told my parents about it. They were horrified, knowing what I did not know— that I could have been violated. All day long the subject of conversation was "locked bathroom door." I sat in the back of the car, sulking and wondering what all the fuss was about.

We decided to explore Atlanta, Ga., on one trip. We had all devoured the book *Gone With the Wind*, and we just *had* to see that town. The people were extremely friendly, but other than that, it was just another lovely big city. When we got to Peachtree Street, it was just a street, but to me it was special. In my wild imagination I could see proud Scarlett O'Hara walking down it.

On our way back to Indiana, we stopped at a tourist home. Our hostess was a widow and she confided to me that an FBI man had slept in our very room the night before. I was thrilled because I listened to all the radio shows about FBI men.

After two weeks away from our comfortable home, we began to long for it once more. Now, when Dad had the urge to go home, home we went. It didn't matter if we were 500 or 600 miles away. Today we think little of trips of that distance because cars are fast and roads are excellent, but back then, cars were not geared for speed and roads were not always good. We sometimes wandered several miles out of the way, but home we went.

When we pulled up into that familiar driveway and looked at our comfortable home once more, we could almost feel its loving arms enfolding us. We would sit around the old kitchen table, sipping Ovaltine. Dad would smile and say, "Now isn't this the best place on earth?" and Mother and I would agree. Looking back at that beloved home, I can still say that it truly was. ❖

Cabins $1, Bedding 50 Cents Extra

By Chris Jensen

"We stayed in such a lovely motel, had a lovely swim, watched the late show, took a lovely shower, then went to bed in such a lovely bed."

This is the standard report one gets today on the average vacationer's accommodations on his trip. Then that subject is dropped with a bored air and a more exciting topic is brought up, such as how many miles the vacationers drove each day.

But not so in the 1930s. Then motel living was an almost profane adventure. One overnight stop at a motel—or "cabins," as they were called—could furnish enough material for strongly worded conversations for weeks to come, and a two-week vacation could furnish material for an entire year. And most of the language used was a lot more forceful than a phlegmatic "lovely."

The first touch of adventure was trying to find the cabins at the end of a day's drive. They were usually located on the outskirts of towns and cities. It was claimed that town councils passed ordinances against having them inside the city limits because of "the class of people" who typically stayed in them.

He collected the dollar before the tourist even had a chance to look at the cabin. Now he didn't have to worry anymore if the hens laid enough eggs to pay for their feed.

Personally, I think the townspeople were simply ashamed to have these architectural derelicts in close proximity to their staid homes and business buildings. After all, Taj Mahals they were not.

You often hear of a building being "thrown" together. These cabins were certainly in that category, and with some of them, the builder must have been a long ways away—and blindfolded, too—when he did the throwing. The architect probably had done his research at the tarpaper-shack village of Hooverville.

Maybe they were located so far out of town because some farmer wanted to make use of a corner of the west 40 that wasn't worth a darn for growing hog feed. Then too, he just might have had a vacant chicken coop. By adding a window or two and nailing up a board sign that read "Cabins $1, Bedding 50¢ Extra," he could be in business.

He collected the dollar before the tourist even had a chance to look at the cabin. Now he didn't have to worry anymore if the hens laid enough eggs to pay for their feed. The unfortunate tenant was stuck, and before morning would realize he was not the original occupant. No amount of plaster or whitewash can hide the fact that chickens have a very cloying B.O. Certainly no one used the word "lovely" with respect to such accommodations.

Cabins were usually built in rows with enough space between to park a car. The number varied, I suppose, according to how much unprolific land was

available, or, as in the West, how much grease-wood and cactus could be cleared without too much trouble. Certainly no one in his right mind would want to use good land to furnish living quarters for "that class of people."

On the average, each cabin measured about 9 by 12 feet—just big enough for a double bed and a chair, maybe two. A number of spikes hammered into the wall served as hangers for clothing. A few "deluxe" models might have a vanity for the ladies—a shelf braced against one wall. The whole thing looked like a theatrical set from *Tobacco Road*.

Many words were used in recalling a night's lodging then, but definitely not "lovely."

And you couldn't use "lovely" when talking about the beds, either. This last summer we stayed in a motel where the twin beds were of the French Provincial period. The beds in those 1930 cabins were of a different period altogether—Post–Junk-Heap.

Those were the days of the Great Depression and thousands of men were out of work. This was fortunate for the cabin builders because it enabled them to have dozens of men scouring the countryside for ancient, crippled, cast-iron beds. These beds had to meet certain standards. The head and foot must be bent so that they leaned toward each other when the bed was assembled. If they didn't, then someone had to pound them into that shape with a sledgehammer. And how fortunate they were if they found a bed whose head and foot *touched!*

It took a great deal of planning and working to find so many bedsprings that were twisted so that you either slid toward the foot or the head or they tossed you off onto the floor. Actually, they weren't really springs at all. They were large pieces of petrified chain mail fastened to a cast-iron frame and carefully engineered so that the sharp edges dug into your ankles and the back of your neck.

How marvelous it must have been for all those people who were kept busy wadding up soggy cotton balls to stuff into the mattresses. Some even gathered straw, and one time they must have thrown in a few corncobs.

Of course, not every spring and mattress was twisted sideways. Some were bent in a "V"

shape in the middle. You didn't roll off, but it was almost half a day before you could walk upright.

Business couldn't have been all bad in the 1930s. Someone sold those cabin builders thousands of yards of faded print curtains for the windows. Some factory must've worked many hours overtime turning out one identical pattern, not to mention the hours of work in laying that cloth out in the sun to get just the right faded look. And how about those craftsmen who so cleverly zigzagged the frays on the bottom edges?

There were no rugs on the floors, but the lint acted as a cushion between your feet and the rough-sawn boards.

No television either, but that didn't mean there was nothing to see. In the West you could look out the window and see endless sand and sagebrush. In the Midwest you might be fortunate enough to see an approaching tornado. And after dark you could turn on the single 20-watt drop light and watch the spiders spinning webs among the wooden beams in the ceiling. Sometimes you could even watch a spider slowly lowering itself towards your wife's bed. When she noticed it, she certainly didn't use any words like "lovely."

But you might even be too busy to look anywhere at all. You might have company, as we did in what were known as the "Leaning Wall cabins." Local tradition had it that the walls leaned toward the east in the morning and toward the west in the afternoon. The sun's heat on the walls at different times of the day caused the bedbugs to rush to the warmest wall, and their weight was so great that it caused the walls to lean. I can't vouch for that, because we moved in after the sun had gone down, but I do know the bugs served as excellent alarm clocks. We had planned to get up at 6, but we were all packed and out of there by 4 a.m.

Not every cabin was built to skimpy dimensions. We pulled into a cabin yard in the Midwest where there were four barnlike structures. When the owner opened the double doors at one end, there was a room large enough to house a small dirigible. Half of the floor was dirt. The other half had a wooden deck about a foot higher than the dirt. On this deck were an old coal stove, a coal scuttle, a water bucket and ladle, an old table covered with patched oilcloth, two paint-chipped chairs and two double beds. The shapeless mattresses and pillows were covered with striped material, scavenged from a chain-gang commune, no doubt. To insure privacy between the two beds, a curtain of that ubiquitous faded floral print could be pulled along a wire with a teeth-edging screech.

"Where do we park the car?" I asked innocently.

"Right here, where it's handy to get at your valises and easy to load up in the morning," he said, pointing to the dirt half of the floor.

"And don't leave those doors open. Last night a hurricane blew one off and it sailed 3 miles down the road." And with that, he banged the doors shut.

So there we were, bed partners with a scorching-hot car, momentarily expecting the cabin doors to be ripped off as a hot prairie wind rattled the building. In the few snatches of sleep I got, I dreamed that the wicked witch in *Hansel and Gretel* had succeeded in stuffing me into her oven.

As we left the next morning, two weary-looking horses were slouching outside the cabin. I detected an accusing look in their eyes. I am sure they must have resented our usurping what had been their former quarters.

For this we should use "lovely"?

A "lovely" shower? Oh, yes, we took showers—not every day, of course, but when we felt we had gathered enough travel dust, we began looking for a place advertising "showers." This usually meant a shower head on a cold-water pipe, outside, and housed in an oversized packing box, open to the skies—a sort of soggy tiger cage. In the hot summer these showers weren't too bad, but in the chill of spring and fall, it might take half a day to thaw afterward.

Not every builder was a competent carpenter, as we found out in a small western town. We came in about 9 p.m. The owner didn't even get up from his chair when we had paid him.

"Take number four; it's open." He motioned down the cabin row.

Dead tired, we climbed into bed for a good night's sleep in preparation for an early start in the morning. We got up, packed and were ready to leave just as the sun was coming up. I tried to open the door, but it wouldn't budge. I looked at the lock but there seemed no way to get hold of it. I pulled; I twisted the door knob, I shook the door, even gave it a few kicks (an unfailing mechanical device).

Finally we heard a gruff, sleepy voice outside. "What the heck is going on around here?"

"I can't get this door open," I said. "There doesn't seem to be an inside knob on the spring lock."

"Oh," said the proprietor, accusingly, "you shouldn't have shut that door. I put on those locks myself, but the manufacturer must have made them wrong. Once you get them locked, there is no way to open them. You will have to climb out of the window. I'll have to get a locksmith from town and that's going to cost me a lot more than I got from your night's rent."

That was "lovely"?

Naturally, it wasn't all bad and it wasn't all primitive. We did have electricity, and by pulling a chain, you could get enough light to find even the smallest suitcase. That, of course, was "lovely."

Nowadays I see "AAA" on the signs in front of many motels. Most of those in the 1930s could have been marked "AA-AA-AAGH!" ❖

Lunch Counter by John Falter © 1946 SEPS: Licensed by Curtis Publishing

Lester's Restaurant

By Violet G. Hepler

Today, as we drive past the large white house that was once my home, I can't help but think back to the days when we had a restaurant there, and remember the bustling activity that went on. The house is located on what once was a busy highway linking many roads to the big city of New York, but the traffic no longer drives by that house. Instead, it has been rerouted to a big four-lane highway that has limited access. If we stop for a moment and listen, we can still hear the hum of traffic and the noise of the big trucks on the new highway, but back here at the house, all is serene and quiet. Off in the distance, you can see the beautiful Blue Mountains of Pennsylvania. I remember how the customers used to sit at the tables, looking at those mountains and admiring the view.

My parents built the house that would be not only my home for 18 years, but a busy restaurant. I was 4 years old at the time; it was during the Depression and few jobs were available. Daddy was not able to get a steady job. Instead he found odd jobs on farms for $1 a day. Then Mom was offered a job at her uncle's hotel-restaurant as combination cook, chambermaid, waitress, and so forth. Room and board were offered to both my parents if Mom would consent to work there.

However, I was not part of the bargain. No matter how much Mom coaxed and cajoled her uncle, he would not allow her to bring me along. So in order to have a roof over their heads and food to eat, Mom consented to work at the hotel. Daddy continued with his odd jobs, which by now consisted of pumping gas at a gas station in the same small town where Mom worked.

Meanwhile, I had been given into the care of my father's parents, who doted on me. My twin aunts treated me like I was a living doll to play with and care for. Needless to say, I thrived under such attention. Mom and Daddy would come to see me once a week, on their only day off. I would go wild with delight and become uncontrollable in my joy, running from one to another, but then they would have to leave me behind again for another week. Each Saturday as the pain of leaving grew worse, Mom would try again to convince my uncle to allow me at the hotel. But he still refused.

Finally my parents decided that they just had to do something so they could have me with them. They had been able save a little from their meager wages and decided they would buy a parcel of land. But they knew that if Mother's uncle became aware of their plan, he would nip it in the bud. Mom was an excellent worker, and losing her would have inconvenienced my uncle a great deal.

But Mom and Dad kept making their plans. They quietly found a plot of land and purchased it. When my uncle found out, he was irate, to say the least, and he did attempt to block the purchase. But since everything was in legal order, he could do nothing to stop it. Mom and Dad were finally on their way to a place of their own.

At first my parents had thought they would have only a gas station, since that was the work that Daddy had done and enjoyed. So the house was built and gas pumps were installed out front in the center of a large driveway. However, many customers who stopped for gas asked if they could get a sandwich and a cup of coffee also. Finally Mom decided to open a small luncheonette, serving sandwiches and coffee. Our living room was made into a lunchroom with a 12-foot counter, stools and six tables. Of course, by this time, my parents had taken me to live with them.

It was still rough going financially. Business was slow at times and the country was just coming into the Depression. When people came into the restaurant, Mother started my training as a waitress. I do not remember how old I was when she first entrusted me to "set the table for the customers" by taking in the silverware and glasses of water. Finally the time came when I was old enough to do all the waitressing.

Mom and Daddy did the cooking and their fame spread. Our restaurant was called Lester's Restaurant (for my father) and many customers who returned summer after summer told us they looked for "Lester's place." We catered mostly to the tourist trade traveling to and from New York City, and one of our first years of business was during the World's Fair of 1938 in New York City.

My parents are Pennsylvania Dutch and Mom's menus featured simple, old-fashioned home cooking. The menus did not offer gourmet fare, but people enjoyed her food—roast chicken, roast beef and roast pork, all made with good brown gravy, and thick fried steaks were some of the platters served. She also made her own homemade soups—vegetable, chicken-corn-noodle, ham-and-bean—all thick with vegetables and meat.

As I grew older, I helped with some of the cooking. My specialty was chocolate custard pie. Mom would make the pie crust. Then she would say, "OK, Violet, now make the custard," and she'd give me verbal directions on how to do it. Mom's recipes were mostly in her head, which, as she often told me, is where a good cook's recipes are. I would carefully do as she told me, then nervously stir the custard—"Keep stirring or it will burn on the bottom."

When it finally suited her, I was allowed to pour the custard filling into the baked shell. Then I made the meringue, again under her eagle eye, and baked it. When a customer asked if the pies were homemade, I could proudly say, "I made the chocolate custard pie myself."

As business grew, it got to be too much for my parents and me, so we hired local girls to help waitress. In those days one didn't work eight hours and then go home. The other waitresses lived with us six days a week, just as Mother had done when she worked for her uncle, with one day off each week to go home.

Our busy times were breakfast from 7–9 a.m.; lunch from 11 a.m. to perhaps 1 p.m.; and then dinner from 4–6 p.m. In between, we would do all the housekeeping chores. Mom would do the laundry and we girls would take turns hanging it on the line to dry and then alternate working in the restaurant and doing the ironing. Cleaning was also done between the busy restaurant hours. And oh, yes—hot summer afternoons found me pushing the hand mower on the big lawn surrounding our home-restaurant.

Sometimes we were kept busy just helping Mom get food ready for the restaurant. She would often make chicken pot pie or creamed chicken livers on toast. When she made soups, we girls had to peel and chop the vegetables. Mom also made pepper cabbage, a Pennsylvania Dutch "sour" made with grated cabbage, celery, green peppers, salt, sugar and vinegar. We peeled bushels of potatoes, husked dozens of ears of corn, sliced pounds of tomatoes, sliced lemons for iced tea, and cut butter into patties. (In those days, the butter did not come neatly sliced and separated with wax paper.) We were kept busy with these chores until the restaurant filled with people. Then we were serving customers again.

During World War II, my father worked in a defense plant while Mom and I kept the restaurant and gas pumps going. She took care of the pumps, although as I got older, I also learned to dispense gas, check the oil, clean the windshield and also, "Check the air in my tires, please!" This was well before the years of "self-service" stations.

Back in the restaurant, Mom did the cooking and I did the serving—and the dishes. Oh, those dishes! I can see them yet, stacked on the sink, mountains of them, every day. I suppose that's why, even today, whenever someone complains about the quantity of dirty dishes after a meal, I never think of them as being many because I remember all those I used to wash after a busy day in the restaurant.

As the years went along, more people traveled and our restaurant got even busier. We began serving between 200–300 people in that tiny restaurant, so Daddy hired an attendant to help out at the pumps and my grandmother and one of my twin aunts came to help in the kitchen. We did finally get a dishwasher, but by then my grandmother and aunt usually took care of that end because all the waitresses were busy serving customers.

The work was really not all that hard, but we were on our feet all day and always busy. We had our good times, though. One day each summer, Daddy would close up the whole place and we would go to a nearby city where we could shop all day. We would close up on another glorious day each summer and all go to Hershey Park in nearby Hershey, Pa., and have a fun time on the roller coaster, merry-go-round and so forth.

On Wednesday evenings, we would go to an auction where people sold produce they had raised on their local farms. Daddy and Mother would stock up on fresh corn on the cob, red ripe tomatoes, peas, lima beans, string beans fresh from the vines, and anything else that Mother could use in the restaurant. And Daddy never failed to get a huge red watermelon. The next day, after all the work was done—dishes washed, corn husked, potatoes peeled for the next day, soup simmering on the stove—in the lull between noontime rush and the evening rush, Daddy would cut that big watermelon which had been chilling in the deep caverns of our monstrous refrigerator, and we would sit around the work table in the kitchen, eat that watermelon, joke and have a jolly time.

I can still see the other waitresses: Irene and Laura, who later became nurses with the money they earned in wages and tips; Rita, with the beautiful dark hair; Carolyn, who was as close to me as a sister, but who died in an automobile accident at the age of 18, a month before graduating from high school; Millie, who was my maid of honor at my wedding;

and Carrie, who is still one of my dearest friends. I can see my grandmother and aunt getting dishes out of the dishwasher and helping with the kitchen chores, and, of course, I see my parents, overseeing everything.

Eventually I graduated from high school, in the same year Route 22 was rerouted. Now it is only a service road with local traffic. Perhaps famous people stopped at our restaurant; if they did, we were not aware of them. However, we do know that the truck carrying Gene Autry's horses stopped for gas one day, and that was a thrill for us.

After the restaurant was no longer in business, my parents built another gas station on the new highway. But we continued to live in our old home, converting the room that had been a restaurant dining room back into living quarters. My parents never operated a restaurant again, and all the equipment was gradually sold off.

I left home, became a secretary and married a young man whom I had met at the farm auction years earlier. My father died about six years ago, and up until a year ago, my mother still operated the gas station at the new location. At the age of 72, she finally retired and sold her properties, including the restaurant that had been our home all those years. The restaurant has now been remodeled by the new owners. Grass grows where gas pumps once stood and a picket fence stands where cars used to park.

The restaurant's original wooden counter and the six bright red swivel stools are now in our summer cottage. When my grandchildren come to visit, I seat them on those stools, get out the milkshake mixer that I used in the restaurant, and tell them how I used to make milkshakes for our customers. I then mix up an old-fashioned milkshake with the still-shiny stainless steel Hamilton Beach mixer.

And when the children have gone home, I lean on the counter and close my eyes, and in my memory I can see Carolyn, Millie and me standing behind that counter, waiting for the noon rush to start and talking about the boys we would meet at the auction.

I still treasure the card a customer took the time to write, leaving it on the counter with a tip. On the card it said, "Thanks—to a very sweet young lady." ❖

NO TRESPAZZ

norman rockwell

You Can't Get There From Here

By June Marie Schasre

Pa was the first to notice the little coin slot near the bed in the tourist cabin. A sign above the slot read, "Massage: 25¢." The fine print promised instant relaxation from the aches of traveling. According to the directions, one simply had to insert a quarter, lie down on the bed and feel "pleasant vibrations."

Pa was vulnerable to vending machines of any kind, and as his back ached from driving all day, I knew he was prepared to part with a quarter. Wishing to get the most for his money, he suggested that the entire family lie down upon the mattress. That meant Ma, all the kids, and Grandma.

When we were installed on the bed in one huge, uncomfortable lump, Pa ceremoniously inserted the coin and quickly joined us. There was a moment of hesitation while we collectively held our breath in anticipation and dread. Then we heard a loud *clink*—but nothing else happened.

Pa got up and pounded the slot machine with his fist. The combination of pounding and cussing brought the manager to the door. Eyeing Pa's wrath, the man gave him a polite apology and another quarter. Pa debated over pocketing the quarter or persisting in getting a massage. We remained crowded expectantly on the mattress, so he decided to drop the coin into the slot.

We never got a blowout when we wore old clothes. They invariably occurred when we were dressed for a wedding or funeral.

Suddenly the lamp on the bedside table began to tremble. The wooden floor shook. Metal coat hangers on the rod nearby clanged together. The entire room seemed to be in motion. A water pitcher on the dresser spilled over onto Ma's leather pocketbook. All the while, Pa peered over his bifocals, trying to read how long a period the 25 cents purchased. The crowd on the bed huddled together, kids giggling, grown-ups indignant, and all envisioning an entire night of nerve-jangling commotion.

Exactly 15 minutes after the coin had been dropped—an interval that seemed to the kids to last forever—there descended an eerie silence as the vibrations ceased abruptly. It was a relief to get into the quiet beds and settle down to a good night's sleep. And we would have accomplished this, had it not been for that second coin

Pa had dropped into the machine. At 3:25 in the morning, some fluke of nature caused the errant quarter to drop down and activate the mechanism, which set Pa's bed to vibrating noisily.

When Ma screamed, we in the adjoining room crawled over Grandma and raced through the doorway to Pa's side. We all piled onto the bed—except Grandma, who did not wish to be electrocuted—and experienced our second massage. Whatever other effects it had, the main result was a very cranky Pa during the following day's traveling.

The next morning we piled into Tillie, the family car. Pa always named his cars Tillie, a custom inherited from Great-Grandpa. As we drove along, we could not help but reminisce about other trips the family had taken in other Tillies.

In Grandpa's case, he usually went 20 miles in the wrong direction before he approached a town he didn't want to be in. Then he'd drive to a new fork in the road with no sign whatsoever.

Tillie took Grandpa's family everywhere. From as early as 1910, when he paid $825 for the new, black Model T Ford, Grandpa was on the go. His trips always featured several flat tires, or as he called them, "blowouts." They made more noise than the bottles of home-brew beer that exploded in his cellar.

The balloon tires had to be inflated with a hand pump that was carried in a toolbox strapped to the running board. When the inner tube was removed, it had to be inspected for a leak and a rubber patch was cemented over the hole. Everyone carried a little cylindrical container filled with spare patches and evil-smelling rubber cement.

Grandpa never got a blowout when he wore old clothes. They invariably occurred when he was dressed for a wedding or funeral.

On a trip to Detroit to attend a relative's funeral, Grandpa stopped at a farmhouse dining room for breakfast. He was distressed to learn that they had no eggs. However, the owner reassured him that there would be eggs if he cared to wait.

"Wait for what?" Grandpa asked, irritated. A long delay might make him late for the funeral.

"For our hens to lay some," replied the man.

"If they can do it in 30 minutes, I'll have some," growled Grandpa.

They did, and he enjoyed the freshest eggs he ever tasted.

In 1921, Grandpa's Tillie became a black sedan. It was a closed-in model with window shades and it sported a spare tire mounted on its side. Grandpa decided to break her in by driving to Atlantic City. He'd heard there was to be a bathing-beauty contest there.

The trip was a lengthy one but well worth the effort. Atlantic City was a foremost tourist attraction, and Grandpa and Grandma had their picture taken by one of those commercial photographers who made it appear that they had arrived over the waves by rowboat rather than in Tillie.

The "bathing beauties," according to Grandma, were a disgrace to the female race. They appeared in public wearing tunic bathing suits and long stockings. Every one of them wore a hat to cover her curls. The one who disgusted Grandma most actually rolled her stockings down to reveal her bare knees, and her bathing suit was much too revealing to suit Grandma.

In 1925, practically all cars were black. Any other color was a novelty, a fact that appealed to Grandpa's adventurous nature. He spent many sleepless nights pondering over the choice he had to make: rich Windsor maroon or deep channel green. There were no other choices in those days, thank heavens, for it took Grandpa a month to finally decide which to buy.

His new Tillie was green. He and Grandma and his kids navigated along at 30 miles per hour. Sometimes he would step on the gas and put her at 40, but Grandma liked to go slowly enough to read the little Burma Shave signs along the roadside. The signs in each set were placed along the roadside at regular intervals, and each sign contained a few words to a rhyme. One in particular remained in Grandma's memory:

Famous last words
For lights that shine
If he won't dim his lights
I won't dim mine.
Burma Shave

Grandpa had almost 2,000 miles on his car when he started out for Niagara Falls a few summers later. The route was teeming with plenty of places to eat and fill the car with gas. Service stations had sprung up like toadstools, and a dollar would buy a tankful of gas. Hot-dog stands were even more numerous, and foot-long hot dogs could be purchased for a dime.

Near Albany, N.Y., Grandpa stopped at one of the popular chicken-dinner restaurants for the evening meal. The chicken was so tough and rubbery that he wrapped its remains in a napkin, added a caustic note, and deposited it in the suggestion box at the door.

That was 1928, the year the summer was so hot that it was referred to as "a real scorcher." While Albany was unbearable, Washington, D.C., was even worse. In a stuffy tourist cabin, Grandpa read in the newspaper that someone had actually fried an egg on the steps of the Capitol in Washington. As he fanned himself with the folded newspaper, I am sure he would have given an eyetooth for a glimpse into the future world of air conditioning and motel swimming pools.

Grandma often remarks that she would have given her eyeteeth for decent restrooms along the way. Back in those days, the only places to provide relief were shabby service-station restrooms, kept under lock and key "for God-only-knew-what reason."

One place in Vermont—a general store with an outhouse in the rear—remains in Grandma's memory. It housed a toilet with one of those elevated tanks and a pull chain. The only trouble was that there was no running water connected to it. The only thing that happened when the occupant pulled the chain was the clanging of a bell, which the storekeeper had attached to the chain for the benefit of the tourist who expected the contraption to "do something" if not flush.

Most of the time Grandpa simply stopped the car by the side of a deserted country road and the kids scampered off into the bushes. Grandma would invariably remark, "Now there will be another lily growing here." I often wondered what the connection was, but I was reluctant to ask.

While air conditioning, cable TV, water beds, hot tubs and heated swimming pools have added to the comfort and ease of traveling, Grandma feels that the greatest innovation of all has to be the improvement in road markings. Years ago, one would come to a crossroad and have to guess which way to go. The weather-beaten sign would simply read "ROUTE 20." Unless the sun was shining or a Boy Scout with a compass happened by, the driver could not guess whether right or left would take him east or west.

In Grandpa's case, he usually went 20 miles in the wrong direction before he approached a town he didn't want to be in. Then he'd drive to a new fork in the road with no sign whatsoever.

Asking a native for directions often proved useless. When Grandpa inquired of a pedestrian how to get to such-and-such a town, the person would invariably say something like, "You just go down a few miles or so to the empty lot where the A&P used to be and turn left. You can't miss it."

That really aggravated Grandpa.

But what really set off Grandma was the oft-heard answer, "You want to get to Concord? Oh, you can't get there from here!" ❖

> *Grandma would have given her eyeteeth for decent restrooms along the way. Back in those days, the only places to provide relief were shabby service-station restrooms, kept under lock and key*

Going to Oklahoma

By Jack L. Feuerbacher

In 1929, our car was a Model T touring car. Pop had bought it second-hand. It had an oilcloth top and oilcloth-and-celluloid curtains you could snap into place in case of rain. The windshield wiper hung from the top of the windshield and the driver operated it by wagging back and forth on the lever put there for that purpose. Pop never learned to drive the car, leaving that to my two older brothers, Frank, 19, and Fred, 17.

Pop got the car overhauled and Mom decided that she wanted to go to Oklahoma to visit her three brothers and other kinfolk. Frank and Fred would take turns driving. On the day we were to start, Frank decided to let the engine "break in" by idling it while we made last-minute preparations. Well, the engine heated up—and up. But Paul, one of my older brothers, happened to go out to the car and shut it off before too much damage was done (we hoped). The Model T had a splash system of lubrication and with the car standing still, application of oil was sort of hit or miss.

We made all of 220 miles on the first day of our trip, so we thought we could make another 200 miles or a little more on the next day.

We got started fairly early and raced down the highway at up to 15 miles per hour. Maybe it was a good thing we couldn't go faster; part of the highway consisted of four rows of bricks, two rows on each side, set the correct distance apart for the wheels to stay on them if you were very careful.

With Frank driving and Fred "riding shotgun," Mom, 6-year-old Buddy and I rode in the back. This was all right, except when we hit a big bump or chuckhole; then we were bounced up and our heads made rude contact with one of the wooden ribs that held up the top.

As we rode along, I thought of a little song and sang it:

> *There was a little chigger*
> *And he wasn't no bigger*
> *Than the good size of a pin,*
> *But the bump that he raised*
> *Just stung like a blaze,*
> *And that's where the rub came in,*
> *Oh the bumped he raised*
> *Came in, came in,*
> *Oh the bump that he raised*
> *Just stung like a blaze,*
> *And that's where the rub came in.*

In those days, an interurban—an electric train—ran between Waco and Dallas. Waco was 110 miles north of Austin, our home, and Dallas was 110 miles north of Waco. Well, about halfway between Waco and Dallas, we had to cross the track. And Frank stalled right on the track. The engine did not stall, but the car stopped moving forward. Suddenly we heard the interurban's horn. Was I scared? You know it!

Fred yelled, "Throw her into low!"

Frank responded automatically. We moved across, and the interurban whizzed past, right behind us. As you old-timers will remember, the Model T did not have a gearshift, but pedals for low, reverse and brake. With all the pedals up, it was either in high or neutral, and you were sometimes surprised or annoyed by which one it was.

By the way, some people have the notion that the old "tin lizzie" got marvelous gas mileage. Don't believe it. Any time you got 20 miles per gallon, you were doing OK.

My sister, Daisy, and her husband, Gene Grubb, lived in Dallas on a wide avenue with double street-car tracks. We got in before dark, which made it much easier to find their house.

About the only unusual thing that happened there was that I saw a bundle of newspapers fall from the back of a truck. I ran out to the middle of the street and carried the papers over to the curb, planning to take them to my sister's house and try to find out who lost them. But the neighbor boy I was with told me that they dropped them on purpose and a boy would pick them up and distribute them on his route. Well, live and learn. Austin was a city of about 50,000, and we weren't very sophisticated.

The people of Dallas had a number of peculiarities. For one thing, they called their city "Dellis." And they used the expressions "believe you me" and "between you and I." Another thing about them: When they drove their cars, they yelled at the other drivers.

In those days, many of the large newspapers carried a lot of funnies. On Sunday morning, my brother-in-law, Gene, would go to the newsstand and get four or five papers for the funnies. Daisy would save all the funnies and about once or twice a year, she would put them in a box and mail them to me and my other older sister,

Florence, who was two years older than I. Boy! Would we have a funnies feast for several days. My favorite funnies were *Slim Jim* and *The Force, Little Nemo in Slumberland*, and *The Katzenjammer Kids*. I also liked *'S'matter Pop? Desperate Desmond, The Bungles* and *Hairbreadth Harry*.

While we were in Dallas, we went over to visit Uncle Gus Feuerbacher. One of the cousins was about my age. It just so happened that his name was Jack, too. He took me over to a huge garage on a vacant lot. It was so big that it wasn't obvious that it had a false rear wall behind which there was a stairway going into an underground chamber. This chamber was empty when we looked at it, but my cousin said some people had had a still down there and made bootleg whiskey. But to their dismay, the police got wind of the situation and sent them all to prison.

Jack and I got along real well, except when I would use the word "temperature." He would correct me by saying "temperatoor."

We made all of 220 miles on the first day of our trip, so we thought we could make another 200 miles or a little more on the day we set out for Uncle John Watt's farm near Okemah, Okla. But we didn't consider the possibility of car trouble. In those days, travelers took along several spare tires, and what a job the old 30 by 3½ with the clincher rim was!

With all our repairs completed, we finally found ourselves again on the road to Okemah. It was just a small village, what we would call a one-horse town. Uncle John had sent Mom directions on how to get to his farm. As I recall it, his cash crop was corn. He also had a bedraggled-looking apple orchard. For fuel, he would go out and find a dead tree, which he would chop up and haul in a farm wagon to his back yard.

He had four mules to work the farm. He also had a little Model T one-seater, in which he and

Uncle Henry had come to see us the previous summer. My cousin Billy, Uncle Henry's son, was visiting Uncle John while we were there.

Uncle John was a Republican, and I had always wondered what one of them looked like. Uncle John could not understand how a town larger than Okemah could exist; Okemah was just about big enough for him and the other farmers round about to market their crops and sell them their necessities.

Uncle John had a well about the diameter of a stovepipe, and a bucket to match. It was about 3 inches in diameter and 3 feet long. I suppose there have been many wells like this, but I have never seen another.

One time my cousin Billy and I ran across a wild plum tree just loaded with fruit. The plums were too tart to eat very many, but we got some sacks and picked plums until our sacks were full. We took them back to the house, and the next day Mom made jam and jelly "until the world looked level," as they say in Texas.

Mom spent most of her time washing Uncle John's clothes, bedding and house. Uncle John was a bachelor and his way of cleaning his plate was to wipe it clean with a piece of bread, turn the plate upside down to keep the flies off, and eat the bread. When it came to clothes, he would buy a shirt and a pair of overalls and wear them until they wore out.

Uncle John had a 5-gallon lard can that he had filled the previous fall with cured bacon slabs and hams, and then filled with melted lard. Mom would fish out a slab of bacon (the hams were all gone), slice it up and fry it. It was a little rancid-tasting, but it beat going hungry. Mostly what we ate were roasting ears.

Uncle John had a little phonograph with a broken spring and a few records. We would play it by turning the record with a finger; we were that eager for some music.

Billy and I were taken to town several times to go to the movies at the Orpheum Theater. We saw a cowboy show and *Smitty* (the funny-paper character), and we also saw a movie about a snowbound bus. (Some years later we saw *Beckie Sharp*, the first full-length color movie.)

Uncle John's house had only two rooms, a kitchen and a bedroom. I don't know how we all managed to sleep; I guess we mostly slept on the floor. So in the evenings, we would sit out under the stars and talk. Surprisingly, Uncle John was far from ignorant about the world. He actually could discuss science, including Einstein's theory of relativity. I was always interested in what he had to say.

After some days, we all piled into the car and proceeded to Okmulgee, the home of Uncle Henry and Aunt Virlie. Billy knew of a spot in a muddy little creek where we could go swimming. But another time we went out to a large dam on Lake Okmulgee. The water was clear, so we decided to go swimming there. We went to the other end of the dam and stripped off our clothes. We had started to wade in when we heard some women screaming and a man yelling at us. So we grabbed our clothes and skinned out of there pronto.

Uncle Henry had an accordion that he could play pretty well, and he entertained us with it every now and then. He also said he could throw his voice, but it sounded to me like he was just sort of squawking in a low voice. Uncle Henry claimed he could not eat when music was playing and if somebody forgot and had some music coming over the radio or from a phonograph, he wouldn't eat until it was stopped.

After visiting with Uncle Henry's folks for awhile, Mom decided to go see Uncle Sam. He lived on a farm, but he had a lifelong ambition to edit a weekly newspaper. Whenever he got a few dollars in hand, he would move to town and start a weekly. Sad to say, he never succeeded.

His farm had no well. Someone had to take a bucket and go to a spring several hundred yards from the house for water. I didn't ask how they took baths, but I supposed that they went into the creek.

Uncle Sam's son Carl could sing real well, and we got a lot of pleasure from listening to him. In later years, Billy got to be a pretty good singer, too.

Billy and I hit it off pretty well, except that he liked to wrestle and he was good at it. I preferred to box. Once when we were squared off to wrestle, he grabbed me by the arm, turned and flipped me over his head. I fell kind of hard and got up angry. I punched him in the nose. He ran to Uncle Henry, and Uncle Henry was pretty upset; Billy was his pet, his jewel. Well, there wasn't much wrestling or boxing after that. ❖

Maine Ho!

By Russ Stratton

Forty hours after my 1922 Lizzie had been transformed through body transplant into a 1927 sport roadster, we were Maine-bound on my vacation trip. It was this small-town kid's first solo tour beyond familiar Massachusetts haunts; filled with pride in my jazzy jalopy and excited anticipation over adventures that lay ahead, I aimed Esmerelda into the northeast at dawn.

Sixty miles out, Esmerelda literally steamed into Newburyport's Ford service garage. Fearful of being victimized by predatory mechanics, I was relieved when a friendly serviceman, fascinated by the automotive hybrid he had been assigned to repair, spotted the problem: an overheated fan bearing. After she cooled down, a fan pulley adjustment and a squirt of oil had us rolling again for a fee of $1, which the captivated mechanic seemed almost reluctant to accept. He wistfully watched us out of sight, loathe to have Esmerelda depart from his presence forevermore.

Driving through Portsmouth, N.H., Esmerelda slowed on sight of two hitchhiking flappers on the drawbridge into Maine. But recalling something about a law prohibiting transportation of girls across state lines, we ignored their fetching smiles and pointing thumbs.

Tenderfoot that I was, and insecure in the companionship of girl strangers, I avoided any risk of confrontation by ignoring hints from the rumble that we park.

Another 100 miles brought us to our destination by late afternoon.

The John Heisers operated the Heiser Studio of Voice and Pianoforte at Somerville, Mass., and "Aunt" Annie Laurie Heiser was my mother's life-long chum. Daughter Hope sang and played professionally, but all her kid brother played was practical jokes. Keith was about my age and we hit it off well on our infrequent meetings. Summers were spent at their farmhouse in Bremen, Maine, hosting relatives and friends, and friends and relatives of relatives, and friends, ad infinitum. This would be my first visit.

When I joined the company, the male contingent included Mr. Heiser, Keith, a Mr. Fogg and me, with "Uncle Gus" and Hope's suitor, Bob Pipe, arriving each weekend. Mrs. Heiser, Hope, Elfrieda (of the Priscilla Quartet, a Heiser Studio concert group), Mrs. Fogg and daughters, Frances and Alice, with Alice's fellow-schoolteacher friend, Polly Fizet, totaled seven ladies.

Energetic Keith proposed an evening joyride, but it was vetoed when Esmerelda chose not to run. A bit weary of travel, I was relieved as well as embarrassed. Esmerelda's disposition was corrected with the purchase of a replacement coil when Mr. Heiser drove to Waldoboro the following morning. Our postponed ride that evening found Keith and high-schooler Frances in the rumble, and the family household chore girl as my companion.

Keith had remarked in passing that Bessie was mildly delinquent, a sort of parolee for some alleged misbehavior. Tenderfoot that I was, and insecure in the companionship of girl strangers, I avoided any risk of confrontation by ignoring hints from the rumble that we park. I kept Esmerelda's wheels turning until it was time to bid Bessie goodnight at her home in the village.

For entertainment, there was a crude grass tennis court, an old billiard table and a rowboat, built by Keith and his dad, which we officially christened and launched in a nearby pond.

One rainy afternoon, the young schoolmarms kicked off their saddle shoes to teach Keith and me to dance. Aided by Victrola music, I managed quite nicely with pretty Alice. It was different with Polly. A bit uninhibited and typically Gallic, Polly was everyone's favorite, her vivacity offsetting any lack of physical beauty. Polly favored

the intimate, clinging, close-packed style of Terpsichore, and I was too nervous and jittery in such a tight embrace to step out with confidence, fearful of stomping on tender tootsies. But waltzing with Polly was a very memorable experience, cheering a gloomy afternoon!

Never will I forget that lobster banquet at the farmhouse! With two chubby crustaceans apiece, plus unending complementary gourmet specialties, our incomparable hosts introduced me to the finest seafood dining. We gorged ourselves until near stupor took over. What a feast!

Another super treat started at dawn aboard a chartered fishing boat. Through a seemingly impenetrable fog, our grizzled skipper inched his craft from one presumably superior fishing site to another, apparently navigating by instinct. I alone caught nothing, my line a target for slick pilferers that repeatedly stripped my hook clean of bait. But my failure to "catch" anything included seasickness, which seemed a fair tradeoff, as all of

Moonlit Car Ride by Eugene Iverd © 1933 SEPS: Licensed by Curtis Publishing

my mates suffered from spells of squeamishness.

Our capable captain was ever listening for fog signals and studying the choppy waters for signs totally invisible to landlubbers. His competence was dramatically demonstrated when the fogs lifted, about noontime, to disclose a tiny island just off our bow. We beached there to prepare lunch over a driftwood fire. Once again afloat, we spent the balance of the cruise in sunshine and comfort, a truly delightful outing.

Thursday afternoon, Keith and his mother informed me that I had been selected to serve as "top banana" at an impromptu Saturday-night vaudeville show, for which each guest was required to prepare a routine. I was no "show-biz" addict, and my apprehension changed to panic when the scenario unfolded. From the skin out, I was to be costumed in a lady's circa-1895 bathing dress, complete with black silk hose, high-heeled slippers, and about three layers of early vintage unmentionables, concealed beneath an ankle-length party frock. (All of these items were exhumed from an attic trunk.)

Appearing at the opening in normal attire, I would contrive to disappear, unobserved, then sneak into the house and put on the costume. Near the entrance of the barn where the crime would be committed, I would crouch behind a stone wall and await my entrance cue, whereupon I was to prance onstage doing a female impersonation of a burlesque queen. Unfamiliar with ecdysiasts and their modus operandi, I pled total lack of qualifications. But my directors, sharing my ignorance, counted upon my innocence to add distinction to the performance. As the closing act, they were sure it would bring down the house!

A sense of obligation kept me from fleeing the premises. No freeloader partaking of such royal hospitality could deny his hosts the courtesy of cooperation in this simple, dramatic (and for me, traumatic) venture. I signed on with distinct misgivings.

And that explains why, in the dusk of an evening in 1929, I sprawled on my tummy behind a clammy stone wall, ready to rise and shine on signal. Finally came John's " And now, ladies and gents, the toast of the Continent, Queenie LaQuiver!"

On wobbly high heels, I staggered into the bright lights within the barn, welcomed by a blast of surprised laughter. In a frantic search for "business" to lend significance to my routine, I skipped and tripped in tight circles around the stage area, strewing flower petals from an imaginary basket in pantomime. Encouraged by the swelling applause, I sped up, adding impulsive little leaps while struggling to rip off sections of the moldy frock.

Cheers and whistles stimulated me to new heights of dramatic endeavor. My dancing to the raspy Victrola rendition of *Makin' Whoopee* grew more frenzied and discarded garments flew, occasionally going so high as to drape themselves over the lofty roof beams. As the last of my expendable undergarments sailed into space, with my spare frame now covered only by the voluminous antiquated bathing dress, the audience's hysteria inspired me to a supreme finale. I launched into a soaring vault, conking my skull against an extremely solid low-slung beam, and I saw stars spurt in all directions.

It was the ideal exit "bit." With my audience rolling in the aisles, my reeling mind summoned up sufficient consciousness to retire, lurching and stumbling to my quarters. To the fetching rhythm of a throbbing headache, the bathing dress was replaced by plus-fours and a polo shirt. My stage debut was finished, and the same could just about be said for me.

Sunday adieus were lengthy and mournful; how sad to leave this Happy Heiser Haven! The Foggs departed some time before Esmerelda finally headed out to Route 1. Just past noontime, moving smartly down the pike, I was startled to see Alice, planted in the middle of speeding two-way traffic, vigorously flagging me down. As Esmerelda slowed to a stop on the shoulder, she ran over to explain, "I swore I'd stop you or die trying!" The odds had been pretty even!

Watching and waiting for me beside a roadside restaurant, the Fogg party had belatedly decided to buy my hosts a farewell dinner, so our all-time final parting left me with a full stomach and a grateful heart. They drove on to their home in Haverhill, and our paths have never crossed again since.

Life is like that. Even Esmerelda was destined for retirement a year later. But never dies the happy memory of those adventures of a feller and his flivver. ❖

Thumbing My Way

By La Monte C. Harris

As I walked south on the road from Carnation, Wash., toward Fall City, hoping for a ride, I wasn't really thinking about anything except the job I was heading for. Looking back, it is absolutely amazing how one small instance can change your whole life. Little did I realize that it would be 32 years before I was in Carnation again.

It was late August in 1935, and I had recently received a letter from my sister in northern Minnesota. She and her husband were farming a place that belonged to one of his brothers-in-law. The letter concerned a job with a farmer at Happyland, Minn., about 7 miles from where they lived, at Littlefork. My sister thought I would have no trouble getting the job if I wanted to come that far.

In 1935, with jobs as scarce as they were, I jumped at the chance for any job that seemed steady. The fact that it was about 2,100 miles away didn't make any difference. Hitchhiking in those days was easy and relatively safe, both for the hiker and the driver.

In 1935, with jobs as scarce as they were, I jumped at the chance for *any* job that seemed steady. The fact that it was about 2,100 miles away didn't make any difference. When you're 19, things like that are pretty trivial; and anyway, hitchhiking in those days was easy and relatively safe, both for the hiker and the driver (though I certainly would hesitate to advocate doing that now).

My first day out went well, even though I did do quite a little walking. I rode over Snoqualmie Pass with a family that included a number of children. I couldn't figure out why they would pick me up, but they squeezed together a bit tighter, and I was able to get in. I rode with these folks almost to Ellensburg, Wash.

At Ellensburg, the Central Washington Fair was in full swing, but I didn't have time for that, so I went right on through town. I got a ride with a fellow who was going as far as Vantage Ferry, a small town on the west bank of the Columbia River. It was hot there, and I was sure glad to get another ride just to get a little moving air. I finally made it all the way to Spokane, but I didn't arrive till well after dark.

The second day was not as good. Since Spokane was a large town even then, I decided to ride a bus as far as Coeur d'Alene, Idaho. I figured that would get me out where catching a ride would be easier. I caught several short rides to get over Mullen Pass, but I was still trying after dark. Finally I got a ride to Superior, Mont. I arrived there at about

1933 International Trucks ad, House of White Birches nostalgia archives

8:30 p.m. and stayed at a small hotel for 50 cents. (When my wife and I drove through there on I-90 in 1973, that old hotel was still standing. But it was no longer on the main highway, as the interstate had bypassed it by about half a mile.)

My third day was uneventful, and I arrived in Butte, Mont., to stay that night. One of the things that impressed me was the height of the chimney on the copper smelter at Anaconda, just west of Butte.

On the fourth day I walked quite a ways out of town before I caught a ride with a fellow who was trying out a new Ford coupe. There is a small pass just east of Butte, and he thought it would be a good place to try the car out. So we rode to the summit. The car performed extremely well, and I wished that he was going a lot farther.

After I had passed through Livingston, Mont., just at the east edge of town, a car stopped me. The driver already had two riders but said that I was welcome to come along. We had gone only a short distance before it became very apparent that he had been drinking a lot more than he should have. After almost running head-on into a gasoline truck, we persuaded him to allow one of us to drive. I was elected.

We went on east, and our former driver fell asleep almost immediately. We had almost reached Columbus, Mont., when he awoke and realized that he was not where he had intended to be. Seems that he had planned to go north from Livingston instead of east. Since it was getting dark and there were no hotels in Columbus, we compromised and drove 40 miles back, as far as Big Timber, where we had seen a hotel. We checked in and left our friend on the street (he was asleep again) to get over his binge.

The next day, my fifth on the road, we split up since we figured it would be easier to catch rides individually. I only saw the others once more, when I passed them on the road.

Not far out of Big Timber, I caught a ride with a salesman for a road machinery company, and I rode with him all the way to Glendive, Mont. We both stayed at the same motel that night, which was one of my expensive stops—a whole dollar.

Leaving Glendive (sixth day), I walked out to the edge of town. I thought that it was really desolate country. The only thing wrong with this thinking was the fact that I hadn't seen the Badlands of North Dakota yet. And I have discovered that the Badlands in South Dakota are far more barren than those in North Dakota.

I made good time until the afternoon, when I arrived in Jamestown. It seemed that I would never get a ride out of there. And that's where I made my big mistake. The highway was close to the railroad, and it so happened that there was an eastbound train taking on water. You know what I thought: Here was a chance to try riding the rails instead of the road.

But in 1935 there weren't any diesels, so I soon discovered that I was going to be unrecognizable from soot if I stayed on that train, especially since I was riding in an open gondola car. The first time the train stopped for a siding, I took off for the highway. I was quickly successful in getting a ride all the way to Moorhead, Minn., just across the Red River from Fargo, N.D. I stayed at a nice hotel there—another $1 deluxe room.

Leaving Moorhead, the next morning (seventh day), I caught a ride with a truck driver. I believe he was hauling dairy products. Just after we passed through Detroit Lakes, we ran into swarms of grasshoppers. They covered everything.

We had to drive really slowly, as the road was completely blanketed with them, making driving extremely hazardous. However, we soon got beyond them and were able to brush the remaining ones off the windshield and out of the radiator. The radiator was almost completely full of grasshoppers and the motor had begun to heat up.

From there we had smooth sailing to Brainerd. North from Brainerd, I was impressed by the beauty of the many lakes. Minnesota is aptly called "The Land of 10,000 Lakes." That night I stayed in a little town called Hackensack. (I am sure that Hackensack, N.J., is considerably larger.)

From this, my final day of travel, I remember large, beautiful Leech Lake at Walker, Minn. It seems to be a favorite lake with many people who go to Minnesota for fishing. I passed through Bemidji and wondered where the town got that name. I am sure it must be of Indian origin, but I've never heard what its meaning is.

After I left Bemidji, the country became more sparsely populated, and after passing through several small towns—Blackduck, Mizpah, Gemmell and Margie—I arrived in Big Falls. When I stopped there to get a snack, I checked my money and found that after all my travels and eating all of my meals at restaurants and staying in hotels, I still had more than $5 of the $25 I had started with. It is hard to believe, but in 1935, you could get a good meal for 25 cents. And the most I paid for a hotel room was $1.

I soon caught a ride that took me all the way to Littlefork, my final destination. I found out that it was 20 miles from Big Falls to Littlefork, with nary a sign of a house or any other building between the two. This ride was number 61 of my trip. I wished later that I had kept the list I had made of all the different cars I had ridden in.

I stayed that night with my sister and brother-in-law and went the next morning to meet the man who turned out to be my new employer. He was a good farmer, but a most difficult person to work for—but that's another story. ❖

Westward to California

By Frances L. Benson

Grandma Rathbun had one wish that had never been fulfilled: She longed to see the Pacific Ocean before she died.

Grandma lived only a block away from us. I spent much of my time at her house where she fed me delicious homemade baked beans and hot, fresh bread dripping with butter.

My dad had grown up in Southern California. His parents and three brothers still lived there, so Dad had promised Grandma that she could go with us on a trip to California in the summer of 1932. It was 1,800 miles from Fonda, Iowa, to Redondo Beach, Calif. In those days that was quite a journey!

When the important day arrived, we all climbed into our 1928 Chrysler sedan with Dad at the wheel. We had great faith in that car with its straight-eight cylinders throbbing under the long, sleek hood. It had carpeting inside, and the beautiful, dark, wooden dash was resplendent with multi-colored lights. I was beside myself with excitement thinking of the grand adventure that lay ahead.

As it turned out, it *was* an adventure. There were no freeways then and some of the highways were just being built. Many of the roads were gravel, complete with chuckholes and washboard grooves. There were many detours, and sometimes Dad had to drive the car at a precarious angle to negotiate a curve. He would have us to get out of the car, and we did—all except Grandma, who said firmly, "If Sam can stay in the car and drive it, then I'll stay right with him."

We stayed the first night in a town in Nebraska whose name really stuck with me—Ogallala. When I almost walked right into a tall Indian dressed in full regalia, I almost jumped out of my skin! He just gave me a benevolent smile and went on his way.

We rented a small cottage at a tourist court for the night. The cottages were square wooden structures with an attached shelter for a car. They all looked exactly alike. They certainly were not built for sleeping! The walls were paper thin; you could hear everything that was going on in the cottage next door. We had the misfortune to be near a couple who fought most of the night. We all arose the next morning still a bit weary and sleepy.

We made Laramie, Wyo., by noon the following day. A rodeo was going on so the town was full of cowboys. It was almost too good to be true! In just a day and a half of travel, I had seen both cowboys *and* Indians for the first time in my life.

On the fourth day, we rose early because Dad wanted to reach Las Vegas, Nev., before dark and we had a lot of miles to cover. I let my imagination run wild when we crossed the desert. Every bleached animal bone looked to me like the bone of some unfortunate human being who hadn't made it across the wide expanse of sand. We had hung canteens of water over the radiator and on the front fenders. But the car never overheated and we used the water only for drinking.

We stayed in Las Vegas that night, ready to begin the last leg of our trip. The Las Vegas we saw was not the blazing city of neon lights that it is now. The population explosion took place between 1940–1950.

Arriving in the Los Angeles area the next afternoon, we went directly to Redondo Beach where Dad's folks lived. We were only a short distance from the ocean and I wanted to take off my shoes and socks and go wading. But first we went to Grandma and Grandpa Zimmerman's house. We went to bed early as we were all pretty tired after our long journey.

The next day we went to the beach and Grandma Rathbun's dream came true. As she stood there looking out across the beautiful sea, she said, "Now I can die happy. I've seen the Pacific Ocean."

As it turned out, it was fortunate that we made the trip when we did. The following year, Dad's mother died, and the year after that, Grandma Rathbun also passed away.

For me, that trip was the high spot of my 11 years. I returned to Iowa with memories that have never faded. ❖

Watermelon Patch by Mark Keathley © Copyright Newmark USA 2002

Against the Elements

Chapter Five

*I*t was the perfect end to a not-so-perfect day. Outwardly, we were the mirrored reflection of this idyllic scene of children helping Uncle or Grandpa gather watermelons. The afternoon sun was warm as we picked out a few ripe, juicy ones for a family celebration. But beneath the tranquility of the scene was the reality of the day's fight against the elements.

It all started innocently enough. Uncle Bob knew the owner of a watermelon patch where melons could be bought on the vine cheap. We often picked our own fruit, from huckleberries on the hillside south of our home to strawberries in the fields a few miles away—fields where you could pick for pay or pick for fruit. So, it was no surprise that we would be going to a watermelon patch to gently thump melons until we found just the right ones.

Uncle Bob fired up the old pickup that always seemed to be on its last leg—but that always seemed to get us to our destination and back home again. My little sister Donna and I piled in with Uncle Bob and we were off on another adventure. Oh, if we only had known!

First there was the obligatory boiling over in the hot summer sun as soon as the motor warmed up. No problem, Uncle Bob always carried plenty of water for such eventualities. Bumping along the country road in a pickup in the days before shock absorbers was enough to make you think you were riding a bronco rather than in a vehicle, but Donna and I laughed and giggled with every buck.

We had noticed the gathering of clouds as we were preparing to leave, but the clouds grew darker and before long the roll of thunder could be heard. Soon the thunderheads swelled and a summertime torrent began. There were no windshield wipers on the old Chevrolet, so Uncle Bob slowed down commensurate with the volume of the rain. Soon slow was too much speed and we stopped altogether amidst drips and streams that took over in the flimsy cab.

Most summer showers end almost as quickly as they start, and so it was with this one. Fortunately, the ignition spark was not dampened to the point it wouldn't fire, so we were on our way again.

The final hurdle to cross before the watermelon patch was a low-water bridge that was now well covered with a swollen stream. As we crossed, we watched the water crowd up the body of the pickup and finally lap at the doors. But Uncle Bob kept the Chevy moving and we scooted up the bank on the other side and on to the patch.

The silver lining was the idyllic scene in the patch and then the tranquil drive home. There were many obstacles getting where we wanted to go on those country roads back in the Good Old Days. But the sweet taste of vine-ripened watermelon was worth everything we went through that day in our fight against the elements.

—Ken Tate

The First Mission Impossible

By Omer Henry

Official records show that *Mission Impossible*, the television extravaganza that delighted millions of viewers, originated in 1966, and the big screen versions began in the 1990s. Not so. The first unrehearsed Mission Impossible was in 1919 for no audience at all in Southern Illinois.

Never has there been a comparable cast of characters. One of them, my mother, wore a soft blue, white-flowered calico dress with a full skirt that reached almost to her button-up shoe tops. In her middle 40s, she was a bit stout, quite religious and deadly serious.

I, a lean, 16-year-old, redheaded, freckle-faced farm boy, was the only other actor. My costume included a white 10-gallon hat with a real leather sweatband, a pair of well-worn denim overalls and a blue chambray shirt open at the throat.

Stage properties consisted primarily of a 1917 black Ford touring car equipped with mud chains, a full set of isinglass curtains, and two pregnant mail pouches; and a cloud-angry sky slashed by imminent lightning accompanied by ear-splitting thunder and torrential rain.

Why did Mother and I stage this spectacular extemporaneously and for no audience? We did it for an eminently sound reason: to make money. Father was a rural letter carrier out of Sumner, Ill., and Mother was his deputy. Even then, a rural letter carrier earned a paid vacation, so by acting as Mom's chauffeur while he was on vacation, Dad and Mom both were paid for those days when she acted as his deputy.

Father was a rural letter carrier out of Sumner, Ill., and Mother was his deputy. On that memorable day in the spring of 1919, Dad was too ill to make his routine trip. As Mom had not learned to drive a car, Dad asked me to drive for her.

On that memorable day in the spring of 1919, Dad was too ill to make his routine trip. As Mom had not learned to drive a car, Dad asked me to drive for her. That gave me ample reason for skipping school and an opportunity for a real adventure.

At 8 a.m., Mom emerged from the red brick post office. A huge brown leather mailbag filled with letters, newspapers and magazines dangled from a strap slung over her ample shoulders. She also dragged a gray canvas mail pouch that contained the day's parcel post.

Glancing at the low, dark clouds, she predicted, "I just know it's going to pour down rain." That was exciting to me! Already the roads were inches deep in mud from a deluge the previous night. If more rain fell, the roads would be even worse!

Postman Soaking Feet by J.C. Leyendecker © 1940 SEPS: Licensed by Curtis Publishing

Anyone with half sense and one eye could see that, in all probability, a miniature flood would begin any minute. "Maybe not," I said, trying to keep the excitement out of my voice. Casually I placed the gray canvas pouch on the backseat and banged the door shut.

"Don't like the looks of them clouds," Mom said, but she climbed into the front seat. I placed the brown leather bag on the floor at her feet and slammed the door.

"What if it rains?" Mom's voice betrayed her anxiety.

"It just rains." I hoped for a cloudburst!

Walking to the left side of the car, I opened the curtains, reached inside and switched on the magneto. I stepped to the front and cranked the engine, listening to its even, four-cylinder hum. Eagerly I returned to the driver's side, pulled the curtains apart, slithered behind the wheel and secured the curtains. Then we were off on the first Mission Impossible.

We were hardly outside the city limits when a blinding flash of lightning zigzagged across the sky and a resounding roar of thunder like a dozen cannons boomed in our ears. I remembered Tennyson's famous lines, "Cannon to right of them, cannon to left of them, cannon in front of them, volleyed and thundered." This was great!

"Lord have mercy," Mom prayed.

For the first few miles the road was surfaced with gravel, so all went well. Then, at Sutton's Corner, we made a right turn and hit yellow mud inches deep at the foot of Sutton Hill. What we needed, it was easy to see, was a mud boat and a yoke of trusty oxen.

"Do be careful," Mom cautioned. Her tone made it clear that she had less than complete confidence in my ability to handle the car.

"If Jesus could walk on water," I joked, "then surely … ." A flash of lightning and a horrendous clap of thunder cut my humor short.

"Mighty close." Mom's tone showed her alarm. "Could have killed us."

"Not a chance." I was remembering my general science. "Lightning never strikes a car. Tires are insulation."

"Don't be too sure."

Then the rain began. Great drops of water spattered the windshield like hail, drummed on the top, slammed against the curtains, turned ruts into small gushing streams of yellow water. A gray haze spread before us, then intensified. I could see barely 10 yards ahead. Huge trees stood like shrouded ghosts on each side of the road, ready to pounce on us.

"Oh, Lord," Mom murmured, "why did we ever start? I *knew* we shouldn't."

Slowly I opened the gas throttle and the little four-cylinder motor roared as its rear tires clawed their way through the yellow mud. The wheels skidded and spun, but we inched upward.

When we finally reached the top, Mom sighed. "Thank heaven," she said, "we made it."

"Sure we did!" I was elated. "Don't tell me you're a doubting Thomas."

Then a wicked flash of lightning splintered a huge oak only 50 feet away. In its wake, a prolonging burst of thunder seemed to threaten still greater disaster. Rain fell in torrents.

Mom turned to me, her face grave. "Let's go back." Her words were a plea, a prayer. "We can't make it."

I wouldn't have turned back for anything. This was an adventure—far better than reading *Tom Sawyer*, *Hopalong Cassidy* or even *Tarzan*.

"Sure we can make it." I pulled up to the Sutton mailbox and stopped while Mom delivered a Sears Roebuck and Co. sale catalog. Then we headed west.

Little by little the rain subsided. But lightning still forked the sky and thunder crashed and rumbled like mountains shifting in a mighty earthquake. Suddenly we faced a graver problem—going down Pickle Hill.

Pickle Hill, a narrow clay roadway cut between two banks of jutting sandstone, was an eighth of a mile long. Heavy rain had carved deep gullies in the roadbed. Enormous rocks protruded perilously from both banks, ready, it seemed, to start a landslide that would bury anyone between those rocky cliffs.

Mom glanced at the roadway, then at the high banks that yawned with their fanglike rocks like the jaws of a science-fiction monster. To her, that pass must have appeared more hazardous than the Grand Canyon.

"We … we can't make it!" she moaned. "We … we've got to go back."

"Go back? After all this?"

"Look!" Mom gestured toward the massive rocks dangling from the banks 20 feet above. "Going between them is like … like riding into … into the very gates of hell!"

"Those rocks have been there a long time," I replied. "I see no reason to think they'll come tumbling down like the … ." I stopped short of saying "like the walls of Jericho." Mom wouldn't appreciate that kind of humor.

"Whole road's washed away," she insisted. "Gone! We … we can't make it! I just know we can't! Impossible!"

"We got up Sutton Hill. Surely we can get down Pickle Hill." I stepped on the clutch and we headed for the bottom.

Again the wheels skidded as the car lurched and jounced. In the valley ahead swirled a clay-colored Amazon. Only the guard rails above the water showed that the 40-foot wooden bridge hadn't washed out.

"Now we're sunk," Mom said, despair in her tone. "Sure as shootin'."

I stopped at the edge of the yellow torrent, pulled on the hand brake, let the motor idle and got out. My feet sank in inches of mud. Ahead lay Pickle Creek, a channel of muddy water swirling at flood level. We were trapped with the U.S. mail between Pickle Hill, which I doubted that the car could climb, and Pickle Creek. And *I* was responsible for that situation. That hit me hard.

We couldn't stay here. Surely we had a better chance of crossing the bridge—if it would hold up the car—than climbing Pickle Hill. Perhaps I could judge better if I walked onto the bridge. I stepped into the water that flowed across the bridge. "Omer!" Mom screamed. "Get off that bridge! Do you want to drown?" She was frantic. Apparently she felt that my weight might cause the bridge to break loose from its moorings.

I walked over the bridge, keeping well to the center. It didn't seem to sag. "Water's only a foot deep over the bridge. I think we can cross," I said.

"Are you crazy?" Mom demanded. "Stark raving mad?"

"No woman is physically fit to run an auto," declared the mayor of Cincinnati in 1908. But, that didn't mean she wasn't fit enough to get one going.

"Bridge seems to be strong."

"Weight of the car'll break it loose, sure as shootin'!"

I walked to the car and got in. "Even so, the bridge'll float. It's big enough to keep us from sinking."

"Don't you ever believe it! And the mail—what about the United States mail?"

"That's why we've got to cross."

"Heaven help us," Mom prayed as I threw the car into gear.

I eased the car cautiously onto the bridge. When the front wheels touched the bridge, it sank a bit. I gunned the motor and held my breath as water rippled around the wheels. Mom, her hands folded in supplication, looked heavenward. In a few seconds we had crossed our Rubicon.

Mom sighed. "A miracle!" she declared fervently. "A miracle straight from heaven. Praise the Lord!"

On we went through the mud. We were near the end of the trip when I

Two girls retrieve mail from an RFD box in the Ozark Mountains of Missouri, May 1940.

Photograph by John Vachon from the American Memories Collection, courtesy the Library of Congress, LGUSF33-001862-M2.

pulled up to a mailbox and stopped. Mom delivered a letter or two. I stepped on the clutch and advanced the gas throttle, but the car only quivered. We were stuck.

"Oh!" Mom wailed. "What have you done now?"

"Hind wheel's spinning. I'll back up." I shifted into reverse and advanced the gas lever. That didn't help. I tried to rock the car, but it didn't budge.

Pulling on the brake, I got out to see how to get the car back on the road. Only a little mud was under the left rear wheel.

"Mom," I said, "get behind the wheel. I can push us out."

"Oh, no!" Mom sounded horrified, as if I'd announced that I intended to commit hara-kiri. "I can't drive!"

"You don't *need* to drive. All you need to do is steer the car a few feet while I'm pushing it. You can do *that,* can't you?"

"I never did." Her voice was far from encouraging. It was as if she felt incapable of such a masculine chore.

"Well, we're stuck. I've got to push us out. I can't do that and steer, too. That means *you've* got to do the steering."

"I'll push. You guide it," she suggested.

"You couldn't begin to push it. It's too heavy. Go ahead, Mom. Get behind the wheel."

Mom looked really worried. Her eyes sent up a silent plea for divine help. "Why," she asked no one in particular, "did I ever try this trip?" But, bless her soul, she got behind the wheel. I breathed a sigh—if not of relief, then of hope.

"Now," I explained, releasing the emergency brake, "when I say 'go,' advance the gas like this." I pulled the throttle down. "At the same time, press on the clutch. That's the left pedal. Understand?"

"I … I guess so." Mom's lips quivered. Her stance and tone said clearly that she felt she was tackling an impossible assignment that was certain to end in catastrophe.

"We'll be out of here in a minute," I assured her. I got behind the car, hoping that my words fortified Mom just a bit. I grasped the rear fender. "Go!" I heaved. "Go!" The motor roared and the car inched forward. It kept on moving as Mom headed it back to the road.

I relaxed, but only for a moment. The motor was still roaring. When Mom got to the road, she didn't stop! Instead, the machine picked up speed!

"Stop!" I screamed.

"Oh!" came Mom's terrified wail. "What'll I do?"

"Brakes!" I shouted. "Step on the brake!" I raced after Mom but I might as well have been chasing Ruttman at Indianapolis.

"Brakes!" I shrieked. "For gosh sake, brakes!" Only then did I realize that I had given Mom no instructions about how to stop the car! Worse, it was careening from one side of the road to the other, spewing a stream of yellow mud from both hind wheels. "Keep in the road!" I cried. "Keep in the … ."

Rural mail delivery in Ledyard, Conn., in the autumn of 1940.
Photograph by Jack Delano from the American Memories Collection, courtesy the Library of Congress, LGUSF34-043270-E.

Too late! In the next instant the car swerved to the right and landed on top of a brush pile, just a foot short of a hefty fence post!

I rushed to the car. Mom was bent over the wheel, sobbing tearfully.

"Oh!" she wailed. It was as if doomsday had come and found her unprepared. "Oh!" Never have I heard so much anguish crammed into a monosyllable.

"You hurt?"

"Oh!" Mom howled. "Oh, I've ruined the car! I *knew* I shouldn't have done it. I knew … !"

"Are you hurt?"

She looked at me with baleful eyes. "Why did I ever do it? I *knew* I couldn't drive!"

I gathered that Mom was not hurt. "You haven't ruined the car," I said. "Not at all. Motor's still running. And you—you did a fine job! Besides, we're nearly home." *Home. End of the trip. Job almost done.* Those were happy thoughts.

"Scoot over." I squeezed behind the wheel, backed the car off the brush pile and onto the road. Mom dried her eyes.

"I'll never try again," she vowed, "to drive a car. Never, never, never!"

It was afternoon when Mom and I got home. Dad looked up from his bed. "How'd it go?" he wanted to know.

"Rough trip," I said soberly. Somehow the idea of adventure was now completely out of my mind. Mom and I had faced a difficult real-life situation and handled it well. We'd carried the message to Garcia, and I had a new outlook on life, a feeling of satisfaction I had never known—a sort of grown-up responsibility.

Dad turned to Mom. "I heard the roads are impossible," he said.

Mom shook her head and smiled. "They're bad—but not impossible." She glanced at me with pride in her eyes, as if she were looking not at a boy but at a man. "Nothing's impossible," she said. "Absolutely nothing!" ❖

Neither Rain, Nor Snow, Nor Sleet, Nor Hail

By Winnie Yager

So many old-timers enjoy recalling the so-called Good Old Days, but at least one woman who lived through those long-ago days grew to prefer more modern methods of mail delivery. According to Laura Tunnell, "Neither rain, nor snow, nor sleet, nor hail, nor gloom of night will stay these carriers from their daily appointed rounds" was indeed an appropriate motto for the nation's mail carriers.

And she knew. The longtime resident of Bristow, Okla., was a mail carrier in the Chandler, Okla., post office. She started as a substitute carrier and then was made a regular carrier when one of the Chandler postmen was killed in World War I.

"I bought a new Chevrolet touring car to use on my route and thought it was the prettiest I had ever seen— until it was necessary to stop during a shower and button the curtains all around," she said.

"Mine was a rural route, and when it rained hard and the mud was almost knee-deep, I drove a team of mules with a little cart hitched to the back. This was in the days when the Deep Fork river in the area overflowed and there were no dams or reservoirs to control the flooding."

Mail carrier jobs in those days paid $75–$100 a month. Carriers filled and put up

1929 Chevrolet ad, House of White Birches nostalgia archives

their own mail, and furnished their own cars or teams. "I carried feed for the mules, as my route was 27 miles long, and with the roads in the shape they were in those days, it took me and my mules quite awhile to make the whole route," she recalled.

Mrs. Tunnell was about 30 years old when she started her regular route after several years as a substitute. It was against regulations to do anything but deliver mail while on duty, but when she was on her own time, Mrs. Tunnell performed extra services and errands for people along her route.

"In case of a real emergency, such as illness or accident, regulations wouldn't count," she said, "but we had few of these emergencies."

Many years later, in the 1970s, a stranger stopped Laura and inquired if she had once carried mail in the Chandler area. When she said she had, he told her that he remembered she used to deliver mail to his parents.

Mrs. Tunnell enjoyed every minute of the work, and regretted resigning a few years short of the required time for retirement benefits when her family moved from the area. "If I had finished my term of required years, I could have been drawing a pension all of this time," she mused ruefully. ❖

Whatever Happened to Running Boards?

By Gail Anderson

Remember when we used to descend regally from our cars? First we would step down upon the running board, then take another step down to the ground. Certainly it was much more dignified than unfolding up and out of our modern vehicles. Whether one uses the bare-thigh-and-garter forward exit or the blind-and-ungainly-rear-end method, there just is no grace or charm connected with getting out of today's cars.

The running board had other advantages, too.

Remember the luggage rack that could be fastened onto the running board, giving additional space for camping gear, dogs and other paraphernalia? The Humane Society wasn't too keen about having dogs ride in such a precarious spot, but there were certain adventuresome canines who actually enjoyed whipping along at 20 or 30 miles per hour, barking wildly at their stay-at-home buddies.

And remember what great sport it was for us kids to ride the running board? In our family, it was considered too dangerous on the highway

1930 Ford ad, House of White Birches nostalgia archives

or main city streets, but for a special treat, we were occasionally allowed to ride the running board down the alley to our garage. Mother would cling to us tightly from her place in the front seat, uttering noises of concern for our safety.

We had a lake cottage, reached by a long country lane that passed through several cow pastures. One of childhood's more pleasant duties was to ride the running board, hopping off to open and shut each gate.

Hitchhikers seeking a short lift could hop onto the running board, then agilely jump off when they got to their destination. No door opening or having to slide over on the seat in those days!

As I emerge from my modern compact car like a crinkled butterfly struggling out of a tight cocoon, I remember wistfully those days of running boards and plenty of headroom. We not only stepped gracefully down from our vehicles, but we didn't have to worry about disarranging hats or hairdos, or (horrors!) knocking wigs or hairpieces askew as we made our exit. ❖

Covered Bridge

*T*oday the covered bridge is one of rural America's endangered species. In days gone by, it was many things to country people: a meeting place; a shelter for travelers caught in a storm; a place to rest in the shade; a place to carve your initials on the huge wooden beams; a place to walk carefully to avoid losing a leg to the dark depths below. And, of course, it was a lovely landmark.

Although the covered bridge may indeed have outlived its usefulness, its memories alone are sufficient to warrant its protection. The following poem, penned by Leon Rawlings, was printed in the February 1975 issue of *Good Old Days* magazine.

> If I could speak through all these years
> And tell of brawny hands that formed me;
> The toil, yet love of labor from those who cared
> To do a job so well I would stand a century.
>
> From inside my heavy beamed walls
> The weary traveler waited out the storm,
> While team stood pawing on the oaken floor
> Until the sun broke through
>   as if the earth's newborn.
>
> Little red boots were stomped
>   free of heavy snow
> As children marched through on winter days;
> McGuffey Reader and Blue Back spelling book
> Were telltale signs of wisdom, soon to graze.
>
> Now, I am a symbol of an age that's past
> No one seems to care about repair;
> The traveler, boots and reader are no more,
> Weathered and old, I stand in stark despair.

© John Sloane

Entertaining Angels

By Paul W. Burres

In the chilly darkness of a spring night in 1925, the rain fell in a steady drizzle and made the surface of the country road slick and treacherous. My wife, Marjorie, my brother and I were driving our 1923 Model T Ford rather late that night, trying to make the 20 miles to my parents' home, and we hoped to arrive before they retired for the night and before the rain made the dirt roads impassable.

We had left the security of the last stretch of graveled road at Abilene, Kan., and hoped to reach the small village of Manchester before conditions worsened. We had gone but a short distance before I had to use the low pedal for every grade. (Model T's had but two gears.) Soon conditions made it necessary to reduce speed to a mere crawl, which in turn made the lights dimmer.

Finally, after we had covered hardly a third of the distance, Old Lizzie slid out of control and we came to a mucky halt in a roadside ditch. It was 10 p.m., not a light in sight. We had never traveled this road before and had no idea where the nearest house might be. I did the only thing possible: I started walking through the mud, not knowing how far I would have to go for help, stumbling along in the rain without benefit of flashlight.

In those years, Kansas farmers had no electricity. But after a few minutes, my eyes adjusted to the darkness and soon I could discern the dim outlines of a house on the ridge ahead. I unfastened the gate and approached the door, expecting the family dog to lunge at me as I knocked. Several loud knocks failed to arouse anyone, so I waded back to the road and trudged on, seeking another probable source of help. After a few minutes I saw a dim light some distance ahead and soon knocked on the door. A husky, friendly looking young farmer greeted me and listened to my story. I was sure he would help.

"I'm sorry I can't help you," he said, "but my wife had a baby last night and I'm the only one here to look after her. I can't leave her." Then, seeing my downcast look, he quickly added, "Back at that house where you stopped you can get help. The old man is deaf in one ear and sleeps on his good ear, so he didn't hear you. Go

back and make all the racket you can, and he'll come out and help you."

I slithered and sloshed back to where the man slept on his good ear and knocked and pounded until I heard stirring inside. I stopped pounding on the door and saw a match flare up. Soon a kerosene lamp drew close to the door. An old man in a flannel nightgown opened the door, listened to my story and invited me in.

"Come in here where it's warm while I get dressed. My horses are in the pasture, but I think I can get them in."

The horses, however, had other ideas! No amount of chasing or coaxing with the feed bucket got the horses any closer to the barn. At last he turned to me in defeat. "They'll come in for feed in the morning. You folks will just have to stay here all night and after breakfast, we'll pull your car out and get you on your way."

It didn't take long for his kindly insistence to overcome my feigned reluctance to accept his offer of comfortable lodgings and a hearty breakfast. Soon I was tromping through the rain again to the Ford to bring my wife, my brother and our luggage to our night's shelter. We buttoned down the isinglass curtains and soon reached the warmth of our host's kitchen. We left our muddy shoes by the door, and after some brief conversation, we were soon in our improvised sleeping room.

In no time at all I was relaxed and warm. I was about to fall asleep when I had a horrible thought: *It's going to freeze tonight and I didn't drain the water from the radiator!* In those days, Fords were not winterized. We often drained the radiators at night and refilled them the next day.

I jumped out of bed and fumbled around in the dark for my clothes, but before I could get dressed, the old man was knocking on the other side of the door.

"What's the matter? Anyone sick?"

"No," I replied. "I forgot to drain the radiator so I'm going to do it before it freezes."

"You go back to bed. I'll go down and do it. You need your rest," came the kind but firm words from the other side of the door. So, while an old man in his late 60s braved the storm and darkness to help some strangers, we—his guests who were in our early 20s—rested comfortably.

We listened till our kindly host returned from doing what I should have done, and then

we slept soundly till morning. We were aroused by the sounds and aromas of breakfast preparations and walked into the pleasant kitchen in our stocking feet. As we sat down to a hearty breakfast of home-cured ham, eggs, biscuits and gravy, we noticed that during the night, someone had cleaned our shoes and polished them.

The horses had been fed and harnessed, so we did not linger longer than necessary over the delicious breakfast. Our host fitted me with a pair of old overshoes so I would not spoil the shine on my shoes, and in a few minutes, with the help of his now-willing horses, we soon had our dejected-looking Ford in the barnyard.

With the radiator filled and the engine running, I took out my billfold to pay our gracious host and his wife for all they had done. But he rejected all offers of payment, saying, "You don't owe me anything. The only way you can pay me back is for you to help someone else who is in trouble."

We started out refreshed and heartened by the kindness of that elderly farm couple. The memory of it all helped us endure the strenuous exertions and the exposure of a long and miserable day. Many times that day my brother and I walked and pushed in the mud while Marjorie drove. Twice we had to stop at other farms for warmth and help. Our trousers were soaked to the knees and our feet wet. Finally, in the late afternoon, it was evident that we were fighting a losing battle against the increasing storm with our declining energies. We turned into another farmyard for warmth and help.

While we dried our shoes and warmed ourselves around the kitchen range, another kind farmer went out into the rain, rounded up a team of mules, hitched them to a topless spring wagon and took us the remaining miles to the warmth of my parents' fireside.

That was many years ago, but I can still recall the warmth of those firesides and the openhearted generosity and help of those good Samaritan farmers. What they did so willingly has left a warm glow in my heart that has outlived the misery of that long day. It has made me recall the biblical verse: "Forget not to show love to strangers, for thereby some have entertained angels unawares." I should add, "In showing love to strangers, often the hosts are angels." ❖

Road Building

By Alice Saunders Mason

My father, Eugene "Gene" Saunders, was born and raised on a farm near Big Tree, N.Y. In 1874, when he was 17 years old, he got his first job on a road, carrying water to the workmen in a tin pail with a tin dipper. Dad got the cool water from nearby springs and wells, and all the men drank from his bucket.

For doing this 12 hours a day, six days a week, he earned the huge sum of 50 cents a week. He told me that he ran all the way home to give his pay to his mother.

Back then, when a new road was built, all the digging was done by hand. Horse-drawn dump wagons moved dirt and stones from one spot to another over the rough roads. The only piece of power equipment was a steamroller, and it fascinated Dad. He'd watched the operator run it until, in his mind, he could do it himself.

One day the operator quit and walked off, leaving the steamroller standing idle in a shed on some farmer's land. Gene climbed up onto the high seat, pretending to run it. When Jim Casey, the boss, who had been observing the lad's antics, yelled, "Can you run it, boy?" my usually truthful father answered, "Sure can!"

"All right, boy. Be here at 7 a.m. tomorrow. Get the steam up and you've got a new job!"

Dad was there at 6 a.m. He gathered wood, including extra for the wood box, and built up a good fire. When Jim Casey arrived an hour later, he was pleased to see steam rolling out of the pipe.

"Good lad," he encouraged Gene. "Now back her out."

If you think my dad panicked, you're wrong! Not knowing one lever from the other, he pulled the nearest one and, with a roar, drove straight ahead through the back wall of the shed and on through the farmer's cabbage patch where, by desperately pulling different levers, he accidentally pulled the brake and came to a stop.

Dad's face was as red as his hair. He expected Mr. Casey to pull him off the panting monster and give him a pounding, but Casey just grinned and yelled, "Seeing you know how to drive so good, get that darned thing up on the road and get to work."

Dad ran that wood-burning steamroller for two years before he was promoted to foreman. He took the first correspondence course in existence at that time, and soon he could read blueprints and handle dynamite like an expert.

He married, had two little girls, and got his first contract to pave the dirt main street through Canandaigua, N.Y. He paved it with brick, as that was the only paving material at that time. The tar used between the bricks was heated in a horse-drawn iron tank with iron wheels. A wood-burning oven on an iron plate under the wagon melted the tar hot enough to fill spouted pails. Men, wearing heavy mittens to protect them from burns, poured the hot tar by hand between the bricks.

The Canandaigua job wasn't easy, as big inter-city trolleys ran down the middle of the road. There was many a fight over whose responsibility it was to pave between the rails.

No sooner was that job finished than he got a contract to pave streets in Rochester, N.Y., in 1905. He did Magnolia, Shelter, Flint, Hawley and Genessee streets. The last of these was a problem, as the city tried a new concept and insisted it be paved with wooden bricks, as they were quieter. And the streetcars ran not down the middle, as usual, but on the sides, next to the sidewalk.

Dad fought bitterly against the wooden bricks, but he lost. He paved Genessee Street reluctantly, claiming that they would split, sliver and chip. They did, much to his delight, as he was a man who liked to be right.

Sick of fighting city hall, he turned to building roads for the state, which he loved, as new machinery was coming into use. He even had a stone crusher right on the road, drawn by six horses, and sometimes pulled out by the steamroller. Until then he had bought crushed stone from the nearest state prison, where the inmates had cracked it as part of their punishment.

By now, I had been born. I dimly remember the road Dad built in Oil City, Pa. He used mechanical donkey dump cars that ran on narrow rails. He loved any new machine, and studied it not only until he could run it, but repair it as well. Included in this contract was a deal to replace the old wooden sidewalks with new brick ones.

By this time, Dad was the superintendent and his brother, Scott Saunders, was his foreman. One day as the two stood watching their men tear up the old walk in front of an old, rundown shack, they were confronted by a dirty, wild-looking old woman who aimed a shotgun at their bellies. Scott took off, leaping spryly across torn-up rocks and ditches, while Dad stayed and tried to explain. But when she screamed oaths at him and actually poked the gun into his gut, he too fled and soon passed Scott.

That night a boy handed Dad a note from the old "witch," as Scott called her. She asked Dad to come to her house, after dark and alone. Uncle Scott begged him not to go; he

Road workers building a bridge in Menard County, Texas, March 1940.
Photograph by Russell Lee from the American Memories Collection, courtesy the Library of Congress, LGUSF34-035634-D.

even reluctantly offered to go with him. But Dad refused and went alone.

Scott was worried about his only brother. He slipped into the bushes and hid in the shrubs surrounding the witch's shack, trying to get up the courage to approach the house. In the darkness, a hand touched his shoulder, and in no time flat he was wrestling in the pitch-black night with an unknown man.

He finally got him down and got his breath back when his violent assailant gasped, "Leave be, will ya?"

Then Scott recognized a fellow worker from the road crew who groaned, "I was worried about both of you, so tailed ya. Fine way to treat a friend!"

With this added encouragement, the two men crept up to the hut and peeked in through the wood-barred windows. They expected to see Dad tied and gagged—or worse. To their eternal disgust, there he sat, drinking cold cider and munching happily on doughnuts and yelling at the top of his lungs into an ear trumpet, explaining his project to the deaf old woman. You can bet it was years before Scott ever told Dad about what *he* had done that night.

From 1915 on, Dad built roads in West Virginia, through Wheeling, Wellsburg and Meadsville. By now, brick roads were being repaved or laid with concrete. Gasoline-operated rollers, steam shovels and stone crushers were common and Dad delighted in them. He built the first four-lane road in New York State on Long Island, and was called a reckless spender and dreamer when he said asphalt was the only thing to use in building roads.

He was, I think, the first man to use an automobile over the rough roads during their construction, but it was an ill-kept secret that when the driving got too rough, he always had a fine, beautiful horse that took him safely over the dangerous spots.

I could relate many more things about this man's years in road building. If I'd been a boy, I'd gladly have followed in his footsteps. This is as I remember him best. The following original poem tells more of the way I feel about Gene Saunders, road builder in the Good Old Days.

My Father's Hands

My father's hands were hard and rough
From work he did from dawn to dusk.
He tore from hills' reluctant sides
The roads over which smooth traffic glides.
No stream too wide his bridge to span,
Up rocky cliffs go roads he planned.
To him, machinery was a joy
He knew, as a child knows its toy.
The harder the problem that tried his mind,
The better he liked it, and covered with grime
And satisfaction from a hard day's toil,
He cared not that his hands were soiled.
Ah! Tender and gentle
   were my father's hands,
To the child he loved—and who loved
   this man. ❖

Oiled Roads

By James W. Riley

Back in the early 1920s, when I was a young boy, we had oiled roads. Each year they received a fresh dressing of oil, and what a mess that made for a week or two!

The small central Illinois town of Lurry had dirt streets, as did most small towns back then. In the winter they could turn into muddy quagmires, and in the summer, they might be topped by several inches of dust. Just a car coming down the street could send up a cloud of dust you wouldn't believe; even the wind could stir it up! Naturally, with no air conditioning, everyone had their windows open, and so there was dust everywhere, inside and out.

In June, the city would oil the streets. This took precedence over the old water wagons that used to water down the streets, a remedy that lasted for only a few hours. Oiling was the way to go.

There were big oil trucks to spread the oil, a heavy, thick, crude oil product that was heated by steam and then spread under pressure up and down the streets. It settled the dust, all right, and the dust remained settled until fall. But what a mess it created! That oil got on *everything,* and as for trying to clean it up, nothing seemed to touch it. It got on the cars and on our clothes; dogs and cats would run through it—or worse yet, fall in it—and then track it onto the front porch. It was bad for the children, too.

After 10 days or so, it would seep down into the dust and create a thick layer, almost like modern blacktop. Then you could drive and walk on it without tracking it everywhere. As it was applied year after year, the roads became like blacktop roads. But each year, we always had to contend with 10 days of that awful oil.

We all cringed whenever we saw the signs that read "Fresh Oil." ❖

A Winter Remembered

By Michael Sproul

To many people, winter is the worst season of the year. It's a time of cold, biting winds, shoveling walks and driveways, and the seemingly unceasing task of scraping frost from car windows. To me, however, winter is a time of remembering—remembering winter as it was on our farm while I was growing up. It was a time of special closeness for our family. The rush and worry of the planting and harvesting was done, and the comparative peace of winter had arrived.

Winter was many things to me. It was going out on a cold, snowy morning to do the milking with my father. It was seeing the cats and dogs come out of their snug beds on the hay and straw to begin a new day. It was seeing the inside of the barn become frosty white from the cattle's breath. It was breaking that thick crust of ice on the cattle's water tank.

Watching it snow was my favorite. I could turn in any direction and see open, snow-covered fields with snow drifting and blowing, sometimes like a dense white fog, obscuring everything.

I guess watching it snow was my favorite. I could turn in any direction and see open, snow-covered fields with snow drifting and blowing, sometimes like a dense white fog, obscuring everything. I watched woods with their trees swaying in the gusts of wind like a dance of exhilaration, while drifts formed everywhere in intricate patterns and designs.

Evening had its own attractions. The day's work done, we would gather in the living room in front of the oil stove. The glow from its fire cast shadows across the room, while in the kitchen, coal snapped and popped in the other stove. They were nice, quiet, cozy evenings spent in reading and small talk.

It would soon be time for bed and my sister and I would go to our upstairs bedrooms. Having no modern furnace system or registers, they were invariably like iceboxes, for the only heat came from the stairway door, which was kept closed during the day to keep the rest of the house warm.

I would quickly get ready and jump into bed under eight or 10 covers, covering head and all. The blankets would be cold at first and I would lie there and shiver, not daring to move until I'd made a warm spot in the bed. But once that happened, what a cozy, blissful feeling it was. I would just lie there many nights, not sleepy, just curled up snug and warm in bed, listening to the wind howl around the house. On colder nights, I would sleep with a couple of layers of clothes on, and on exceptionally cold nights, we would all drag our mattresses and covers to the living room and sleep huddled in front of the fire.

But of all the winters, there is one that has special meaning to me. I was 18 then and working the second shift in Lima, Ohio. My sister was married, and my mother had taken a job in Lima, too.

One morning Dad called upstairs, waking me, to tell me to look outside. The first snow was coming down in large, white flakes. According to the weather forecast, however, it was to end soon, with little accumulation,

In the few hours before I was to leave for work, I paid little attention to the snow, but I noticed that it was starting to stick. It wasn't until I had left for work that I realized just how bad it had gotten. The roads were buried, drifts were piling up and I was having trouble getting through. Deciding to go back home, I made a circle rather than stopping and trying to turn around, for I knew that if I stopped, I wouldn't get started again.

But turning back onto our road, I became hopelessly stuck where I had passed through just 10 minutes earlier.

First Snowfall by John Slobodnik, House of White Birches nostalgia archives

There was nothing left to do but walk the 2 miles home. I was exhausted and all but frozen by the time I trudged into our yard, but I still had to get the car out. After firing up the old John Deere, Dad and I putted our way to the car. I couldn't believe how bad it had gotten. Even the tractor was having problems with the drifts.

When we came within sight of the car, we found two more cars and a truck stuck in what had now become an all-out blizzard. Dad had to pull me all the way home and we barely made it. There was no doubt about it; we were snowbound.

While I was thawing out in the house, my mother called to let us know she had safely reached my sister's home so everything was all right. We had plenty of food and everything we needed in the house. We could relax and enjoy the snow.

There's something about being snowbound—the quiet, the feeling of isolation, the falling snow. There was no electricity and eventually the phone went out. But the fires burned merrily, and our kerosene lamps flickered and glowed, giving the room a warm, yellow light. It was as if we had somehow slipped into the past, before the rush and hubbub of our present era.

Dad and I sat and talked as we hadn't in years. We spoke of my hopes and dreams, of my father's past. That night I found out things I'd never known about my father and my ancestors. I felt closer to my father than ever before.

When we got up the next morning, the snow had stopped, but we were really snowed in! We didn't care. Our feeling of closeness from the night before was still with us. We spent most of the day outside, doing chores and walking to a farm down the road where we kept calves. We saw animal tracks on our way, the only tracks except our own. The unbroken expanse of snow extended as far as we could see.

Although it was late that afternoon, it seemed all too soon that the snowplows bucked their way through the drifts, bringing with them the onrush of modern civilization. Our isolation was ended, but the experience my father and I had shared would be with us always. ❖

Pages 150 & 151; © *City Sidewalks, Busy Sidewalks* by Dave Barnhouse/Hadley Licensing 2003

The Lantern

By Ed Henry

About 2,300 years ago, the story goes, a man shuffled barefoot along the streets of Athens. He was unshaven and dressed in rags. Although it was broad daylight, he carried a lighted lantern in his hand, but history fails to tell us whether or not he found the honest man he was seeking.

Perhaps a man who shunned convention, slept in a bathtub and drank water from his hand might be considered a bit queer by his fellow-men, yet he had one redeeming feature: He had a lantern. This sets Diogenes apart in history as a man of discernment and perception.

No doubt there was little similarity between the light piece Diogenes carried and the barn lantern with which we grew up, yet the coal-oil lantern itself is now an antique. Does no one but me hold a fondness for that old relic, the dispenser of light and warmth? Am I the only person now living who grew up with a lantern as a close companion?

How well I recall the night we came down Steamboat Mountain with the aid of the faithful lantern. The entire family had embarked on a questionable but highly exciting trip early that morning. After a day of bliss, we piled into the Model T in plenty of time to allow for safe passage down the mountain before dark.

Only a fool would have done otherwise. The mountain road was that in name only. The times were too nearly akin to those of the horse-and-buggy days to allow for refinements on the roadways. The Steamboat Mountain road was no exception. In fact, it was a prime example of the other extreme.

Only the long-legged Model T could straddle the high centers, and it had difficulty negotiating the hairpin curves. On one side was the mountain, rearing straight up into the wild blue yonder. On the other side was the brink of eternity. But, true to its nature, the Ford refused to function. The timer was damp, or the coils on the verge of collapse, or some other ailment too commonplace to recall had caused the car to stall.

By late afternoon, by dint of much perseverance and persuasion, Dad had the old bus ready to roll again. While Mother complained about the growing lack of sunlight, Dad eased the quivering Ford down the nightmarish road. Night came on as we jolted along. Then the lights went out.

Investigation showed that the bulbs were burned out and the two spares soon suffered the same fate. By some unknown prompting, Dad had brought along the lantern, and now we secured it to the radiator with the ever-present hay wire.

Feeble as the conventional headlights were, they were brilliant in comparison to the yellow glow cast by the lantern. Where previously we had bounced along at the breathtaking speed of nearly 10 miles per hour, we were now reduced to a snail's pace.

When headed into an outside curve, it was extremely difficult to determine where the road ended and eternity began. One time Dad tramped on the brake and reverse pedals simultaneously, clawing for the emergency with his left hand. The Model T shuddered to a stop, hiccuped a couple of times and died.

"Get out and block the wheel," Dad ordered. I climbed out while my two sisters volunteered advice in shaking voices.

The Ford had come to rest with the left front wheel within inches of the brink of the canyon. I tossed a rock over, and after an age I heard a distant crash as it struck.

Dad got the machine going again and managed to back away. We proceeded on down the mountain safely, guided by the faint circle of light, and when we drove into the shed at home, it was surprising how much light that old lantern gave! ❖

1906 ADAMS-FARWELL had an unusual rotary air-cooled engine rated at 45 hp. The control lever could be moved inside the car for driving in bad weather.

Today as Yesterday—

Cars run their best on the best gasoline

1953 MERCURY offers the widest color choice in its field, plus a high-performing V-8 engine rated at 125 horsepower. New double-stop doors are handy in close quarters.

In 1906—the year of the great earthquake and fire—only about a thousand cars roamed the streets of San Francisco. In fact, there were only about one hundred thousand cars in the entire country.

But car ownership quickly soared as steamers, electrics and gasoline buggies competed for public favor. The gasoline car finally won out because of its dependability and promise of greater power.

That promise has been more than fulfilled in today's automobiles. The combination of a modern high compression engine and today's high octane "Ethyl" gasoline delivers power and performance that weren't even dreamed of in the early 1900's. For the best performance of *your* car, stop at the pump with the "Ethyl" emblem.

"ETHYL"
TRADE MARK
ANTIKNOCK COMPOUND
ETHYL CORPORATION

ETHYL
CORPORATION

New York 17, New York
Ethyl Antiknock Ltd., in Canada

1926 KISSEL was the first of this well-known line of cars featuring an eight-cylinder engine. It developed 63 horsepower to push this speedster along at eighty-five miles an hour.

1915 BRISCOE was a "Cyclops" of the highway with its single headlight. It sold for $785, equipped with a 16-hp., four-cylinder engine.

Lap Robes

By Helen LeMunyon

When I was a young girl, in the early 1900s, no pleasure car was considered complete without a lap robe, usually two if it were a two-seater—a large one for the backseat and a smaller one for the extra passenger in the front.

Cars in those days were not equipped with heaters and air conditioning; such modern accessories would have accomplished little anyway. We had the air conditioning, all right; in most cases, passengers rode exposed to the elements with only the protection of some type of fabric top, and that often creaked and swayed so much in the wind that it was considered safer to fold it down while en route.

For protection in cold weather and when a sudden shower came up, we had side curtains. These were usually constructed from something like plastic, but it wasn't plastic. I think it was called isinglass, and the clear material extended only far enough to make peek holes on each side. The balance of the curtains were made of a kind of black oilcloth with a series of slits or openings that were supposed to match buttons on the frame of the car itself.

Since cars had no trunks in those early days, side curtains were usually kept under the cushion of the backseat. When a sudden shower came up, the car had to be stopped while the car top was raised and the side curtains were hauled out and buttoned in place. Think what a scramble that caused!

In many cases, the storm was over by the time everything was set to resume the journey. In that case, the curtains were usually unbuttoned again and returned to their spot under the backseat cushion, for they obstructed the driver's vision. It was really unsafe to drive with them in place, and we didn't do so except in an emergency.

Under these conditions, it's small wonder that lap robes were used, winter and summer. Winter lap robes might be anything from a bed blanket or quilt to a real fur robe, for those rich enough to afford it.

My family used a heavy bed comforter in the backseat. It was large enough to cover all the backseat passengers' laps and legs at the same time. It was left in the car at all times, neatly folded, and when we were about to take a spin, everyone had to get seated so that the robe could be tucked in around everyone at once. If the

My older brother took this photo with a homemade box camera. Although the photo was not taken in the winter, it can readily be seen that lap robes were a necessity in such a car, especially in cold weather. My father and mother, James and Lena Smith, are in the backseat with me, Helen Smith. Big sister Florence is seated in the front with her husband and son, Elmer and Homer Borland. This car belonged to Elmer.

journey was to be a long one or if the weather was extra-cold, heated bricks or stones were wrapped in rags and placed at the passengers' feet, under the robe.

Small children sometimes presented a problem, as they did not like being obliged to sit still to keep the robe in place. Those who were too active sometimes were made to sit on a box or low stool on the floor, where they could use the bottom edge of the robe as their cover. As a special treat, they might be allowed to sit up front beside Dad or Big Brother who was doing the driving. In that case, they had their own smaller robe.

Mom's paisley shawl was often pressed into service as the front-seat robe in our first car. It was not left in the car, though. It was brought into the house to serve as a living-room couch cover during the week, and as a light wrap on Saturdays when Mom hitched up old Dobbin and drove to the nearest village to trade her butter and eggs for the store goods our family could not raise on the farm.

That paisley shawl was a beautiful, hand-woven affair. I'd love to have it as an heirloom, but as I remember, it was used for so many things that it was worn to shreds. In its final days, it was pressed into service as a warm covering for disowned or sick chicks and other such baby farm animals that had to be brought into the house. They were bedded down behind the kitchen stove till they either died or regained their strength so they could be put back with their peers.

I don't know when robe rails came into existence, nor do I remember if they were already in the car when purchased new or if they had to be purchased and installed later. I do know that

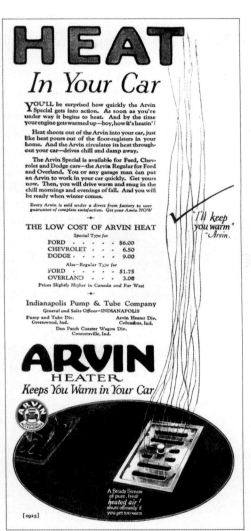

Arvin Heater ad, House of White Birches nostalgia archives

we had a couple of cars that boasted robe rails, which were a length of rod attached across the back of the front seat. Lap robes could be thrown over the robe rail when not in use, thus freeing the backseat to hold picnic baskets, groceries, suitcases and the thousand-and-one items that had to be carried there before trunks became a part of cars' design.

Lap robes were used in summer, too, back in those days, and no wonder. The clouds of dust raised by auto traffic on unpaved streets and roads made some attempt at protection a necessity. Summer lap robes were much lighter in weight, though, usually made from linen (which shed the dust better) or lightweight cotton fabric. The ladies also wore large, protective hats or bonnets, as well as scarves in which they swathed their neck and upper body when out for an auto ride. Men usually wore straw hats and long, lightweight coats called "dusters."

I'm certainly not advocating going back to the conditions of the Good Old Days in every respect, but I'm sure a lot of energy could be saved if we adopted some of the habits of our forefathers in operating our modern cars—and we would likely be the healthier for it.

For instance, couldn't we get along without turning on the air conditioner in many instances? I turn it on automatically now, mostly as a matter of habit. Maybe we should go back to carrying lap robes in our cars, too, instead of turning on the heater, whether we really need it or not. Why not give it a try and see if it wouldn't make a worthwhile difference? ❖

Old Cars & Deep Snow

By Hugh Smith

We grew up on a small farm 10–12 miles from the Straits of Mackinaw in the upper part of Michigan's Lower Peninsula. Our place was 30 miles from Cheboygan in Cheboygan County and 4 miles from Onaway, which was our mailing address. My father, Otto Smith, was a product of the lumber camps, as my grandfather had been a logging contractor. Our mother was the daughter of an Irish farmer and was born in Waverly Township of the same county. Stair-stepped in age were four boys: Clyde (the eldest), Claude, me and Harvey.

When most of the virgin timber had been cut by the early 1920s, our father quit lumbering as a steady thing and went to work in the big sawmills around Onaway. Finally he went to work in the big Lobdell-Emery Wood Rim plant in Onaway. This company made all the wooden car steering wheels for the whole United States as well as most of the wooden bicycle rims. They also made the aluminum (spider) or the hub and spokes and assembled the whole steering wheel. I'm sure old-timers will remember some of those steering wheels. Some even tipped or tilted up out of the way; they were quite elaborate. At that time the town had a slogan: "Onaway Steers the World."

We stopped and watched, commenting in disbelief; we had had an unusually severe winter so far and it was our general opinion that nobody in his right mind would tackle that road with a car.

But the plant burned in 1925 or 1926, putting 5,000 people out of work. They transferred the operation to Alma, Mich., and my father was among those who followed them there to work. He came home on weekends whenever he could.

We lived on a north-south county road 2¼ miles from the highway—M-10, as it was called then. Our road was plowed only periodically, while the highway was plowed regularly, giving us a combination of 2¼ miles of road that was impassable for a car in winter, and

Cars images on pages 156–159 from Vintage Ford ad, House of White Birches nostalgia archives

2 miles that was all but impassable for horses and sleds. That's where the old cars came in.

Our father had a Model T. He became quite adept at coaxing, pushing, pulling and just plain cussing his flivver through snow that most people in those days considered impassable.

Many of our neighbors had cars, including Chevrolet 490s, at least one Buick, an Overland, Willys, Star, one big Chevy (at one time the "big" Chevy 6 was one of the biggest cars), Maxwell, Hupmobile, Dodges and Rios. (Jud Skowten of Cheboygan used Rios for taxi service between Cheboygan and Onaway, Petoskey, Roger City, etc. The last I heard, about 1931, the current one had over 200,000 miles on it and was still going.) However, for every car of another make, there was at least one of Henry Ford's "T's."

Among the advantages of the Model T in the snow were its light weight and the lack of encumbrances. You could stick a fence post, pole, plank or most anything under any corner and prise up the axle and put blocking under the wheel or wrap a tie rope, line strap or light chain around the tire. Often, if it was a touring car, the tie-down straps for the top came into play here; or, if you had them, which we often didn't, you could simply put on the tire chains.

Another advantage was the way you could rock those flivvers. You pulled back the high lever, put one toe on the forward pedal, the other on the reverse, gave it a little throttle and push on the pedals alternately, rocking forward and back a little farther each time until you had gained room enough for another run. My brothers and I developed this strategy into a fine science with all our cars, though with none as successfully as with the T.

The T's other advantage, of course, was the high wheels and clearance beneath, which is all-important in snow. All cars at that time had good

clearance and high wheels. Some of the bigger cars had the advantage of power, speed and a second gear, which gave good speed plus reserve power to carry you through tough going. The Buick was one of these. Its weight, sheer brute strength and speed made it almost unstoppable.

Perhaps one of the best early cars in snow was the Star. It was not big, but it seemed to have just the right combination of power, speed and maneuverability to do the job. I later owned three different Model A's, and though they were generally considered the best yet in snow, I'd still put my money on the little Star.

When our country road became impassable and our father had to go to Cheboygan or somewhere else to work, my oldest brother harnessed the horses and hitched them to the sleighs, and we followed my father until he could go no farther. Then we took the horses and pulled the car to where he could go under his own power again. We repeated this until we got him to the highway, where he'd go his way and we'd turn to return home. When our father returned, if it hadn't drifted in the meantime, he could usually make it in alone. If not, we simply reversed the procedure.

If the road was too bad, we just took a couple of planks and ran the flivver up onto the hayrack, tied it down and hauled it out to the highway.

When the county finally plowed the road, they had big, single-wheeled Dodge-Graham trucks with heavy tire chains. They put two of them in tandem behind a mammoth plow and they'd hit the drifts at low speed, nearly full throttle, go perhaps 5–15 feet, back up and hit it again and again until they busted through and could go on to the next drift. In hitting these drifts, if one of the drivers failed to release his clutch right at or just before the time of impact, the result was often a broken axle, which meant that those trucks, especially if it happened to be the rear one, were to sit there perhaps for days until a rescue crew could

dig them out and make repairs. As for the banks they pushed up, I had occasion once in the 1930s to stand on a truck bed alongside one of them. I could just reach the top, which meant about 12 feet of nearly vertical snow bank.

One of these county plow operators, Lloyd LeDuc, was a friend of the family, so a couple of times he allowed me to get up in the cab and ride to the end of his run, which ended 3 miles beyond our place and back. Well, you may imagine how exciting that was. I don't think my first plane ride or my first long trip was nearly as thrilling as sitting up there and seeing firsthand something I had only been able to watch, open-mouthed, from a distance.

One winter, about 1927 or 1928, our father was working in Grand Rapids. We expected him home for Christmas, though we didn't know when he'd arrive. Well, a couple of nights before Christmas, we boys, with some neighbor boys and girls who all attended Waverly No. 1 school with us, hitched up our horses to the farm sleighs, put on the hayrack and a couple of feet of loose hay, and took a hayride 3 miles west to Waverly No. 2 school to see their Christmas program. (The girl who later became my wife, Fern Riegle, attended Waverly No. 2.)

When the program was over, we started home. We had come to the Tower Road when we saw powerful car headlights coming from toward the highway. These headlights swayed, dipped, rose and fell, alternately lighting the drifts, tracks, ditches and fences, accompanied by powerful rumbling and lots of flying snow.

We stopped and watched, commenting in disbelief; we had had an unusually severe winter so far and it was our general opinion that nobody in his right mind would tackle that road with a car. After all, there had been excessive snow and drifting, and no traffic except horses and sleighs, which cut a much narrower track than a car and really were more of a hindrance than a help.

Well, you can imagine our amazement and excitement when the car finally pulled up to us and our father climbed out from behind the wheel, dressed in a blue serge suit, white shirt and oxfords. He had given a ride to a neighbor who worked with him and who lived on that road.

After the excitement had died down somewhat (for my father was well-liked by all the neighborhood kids), some of us piled into the car and went on ahead of the sleighs. There were two bad hills in the 2 miles home, and we all had to get out and push a few times. Of course, we got plastered with flying snow from the tire chains, but we wouldn't have missed it for anything.

When we got to our drive, which was impassable, we left the car there and took the horses home. Then we took a chain back to the car, hitched up the team and pulled the car to the barnyard. The horses found this was something different than pulling the Model T, which was lighter by some 1,500 pounds.

The next few days we had lot of company. Kids came with their sleds or skis as just over our line fence was a pretty good coasting hill. Some grown-ups came by, too, and everyone had to inspect and admire the "new" car. Actually it was 1923 vintage, but it had been so well cared for by its former owner that it looked like new. In those days, cars were built to last. I've seen cars used by one owner for up to 15 years; 10 years wasn't at all unusual. It was customary then when someone got a new car for all the neighbors to go and admire it, comment on its fine points and any new innovations, listen to it run and, hopefully, even take a ride in it.

This car was a 1923 Oakland, and in our country, it was quite a sight. It was a touring model, long, low and streamlined. It had a permanent winter top: side enclosures attached with screws and consisting of sliding, overlapping plate-glass panels mounted in grooves so that any one could be slid and anchored in any position with a rubber-tipped thumb screw. The

color was robin's egg blue; the wheels were solid disks, and the radiator cap was adorned with a statue of a discus thrower—a real mean thing if you should hit a pedestrian.

Those disk wheels, with the exhaust pipe ending squarely between them, gave this car a peculiar rumble. On a quiet evening we could identify its sound up to 3 miles away.

This car stayed with us for three or four years and it turned out to be a real good snow car; it had power, speed, weight and what we called a good second gear for snow. We busted many a drift in those days that would make your modern-day sport with a muscle-bound four-wheeler stop and scratch his head.

As we approached a drift, we'd size it up for depth and width, already knowing how hard it was. (If a drift had been there long, especially in extremely cold weather, it would be very hard. I've seen the horses walk on them without breaking through.) Then we'd shift to second speed and hit it with whatever speed was necessary, giving more throttle once we were into it. If we misjudged and lost control, we might turn crosswise; then we either had to shovel it out or get a pull with some neighbor's horses.

Also, as soon as we got through one of these drifts, we had to go around and pull the snow away from the radiator or the water would boil out. There was no antifreeze then, at least not out on the farms. We simply started the old bus, made sure it was running good, then filled it with warm water. We then covered the radiator or partly covered it with a burlap bag or something similar and adjusted it whenever necessary to achieve a temperature somewhere (anywhere) between freezing and boiling. I think it was the Hudson that later came out with fins in front of the radiator that you could adjust for whatever temperature you wanted.

All this struggling with cars in the snow may sound strange to some of you, but maybe I can explain it this way:

Our mother, having been a schoolteacher, believed in education. She insisted that all of us complete our high school diploma at least. Three of us did finish high school at Onaway. The oldest, Clyde, went on to County Normal and taught for several years, went from that to the Wayne bank, from there to the Chrysler Motor Corp. payroll department and from there, set up his own business service in Traverse City, Mich. It was doing very well when he took sick and died in 1967.

Our farm was on two 40-acre tracts, one having about 30 acres of wood lot. Now, 50-odd acres of only fair land wouldn't support a large family, even if it was well farmed—and our father was not a good farmer, so there had to be something else going on all the time. When he quit the factories he turned to cutting pulpwood, cedar posts and grape sticks, Christmas trees, cedar boughs and excelsior wood (poplar), and he built and ran a small sawmill for such saw logs as he and the neighbors cut. This, with our going 4 miles to school, involved a lot of transportation. We drove to high school and rode with neighbors when roads permitted, drove the horses through the woods and across open fields when they weren't being used for work, and, as a last resort, we used skis that we made from birch, sawed on our own mill and hand finished. We steamed these so that when placed on the ground, the center arched 2–3 inches above the ground. This allowed us to lift our foot almost naturally without lifting the ski. We could travel at a very good speed for a long way without getting too tired.

All four of us boys were more or less mechanically inclined; I think the snow presented a challenge that we couldn't resist.

I guess that explains it, because if I could, even after all these years, I would still love to get out ahead of the plows after a bad storm and bust a few drifts, just to see the snow fly. ❖

The Rumble Seat

By V.G. Benson

The rumble seat has vanished from the scene and I, for one, say "Good riddance!" There are those who mourn its passing. Without exception, these are people who, over the intervening years, have thawed out and gotten the dust out of their hair. They mourn a dream, not a reality.

Dust-covered magazines retrieved from attics still portray advertisements of cars with rumble seats. In these advertisements, the car always rests on a green lawn, and the rumble seat contains a handsome young man and a pretty girl. They are waving—not calling for help, just waving. The young man is bareheaded, his hair neatly combed. The girl is wearing a large hat; both are smiling.

In a real rumble seat, at any speed over 10 miles an hour, the hat would be snatched from the young lady's head; the young man's hair would look somewhat like a broken bale of straw, and continued smiles would result in a mouthful of dust.

Rumble seats, for the uninitiated, were placed in the turtlebacks of coupes and convertibles. A lid lifted up from the turtleback and, when upholstered with imitation leather and springs, formed the back of a seat. An unbelievably uncomfortable seat was installed inside. It was a narrow seat but it could contain two ordinary people or one fat lady and a cat.

Entering a rumble seat was no small matter. A small round step was installed on the left rear bumper. Another round step was installed on the top of the left rear fender. Rumble seats were, obviously, designed for the young, for entering them required the agility of a mountain goat. Leaving them was no easier, and this was further compounded by the fact that two hours' exposure to the elements left the occupants stiff and numb. Legroom was inadequate and was further complicated by the presence of jacks, tire chains, rubber boots and empty bottles.

While the rumble seat was no joy to occupy while the car was standing still, it was only when the car was in motion that its full import could be realized. Here the weatherman's theory of the wind-chill factor applies. Riding in a rumble seat when the temperature was 50 degrees and the car was traveling at 60 miles an hour left the inhabitants shivering at what felt like a frosty 10 degrees below zero.

Aside from the windchill factor, dust was always a problem. The rumble seat coincided with unpaved roads and other roads so narrow that meeting another car involved driving with one wheel in a bar pit. Nor was this ordinary or garden-variety dust, for it contained cinders, small shards of metal, bits of rubber, oil (both hot and cold), stones and a variety of unidentified objects. Added to this was the dread possibility of thrown objects, like ancient and venerable eggs, overripe fruit and bags filled with water. Some people just hated a sport.

Even on wide paved roads, the rumble seat offered little pleasure, for the wind whipped around the enclosed portion of the car, hats disappeared, ties whipped frantically and conversation was impossible.

To all this injury was often added insult. One cold January night we became desperate. Our pleas to slow down to 10—not 10 mph, but 10 below zero—had been ignored. The cold and wind became unbearable. Searching amid the debris in the rumble seat, we retrieved two pillowcases. They were quite dirty and had possibly been used to transport bootleg whiskey, for they contained bits of glass. Nonetheless, we carefully pulled them over our heads and basked in the delicious warmth.

Our triumph was short lived, however, for a highway patrolman followed us all the way to town. He thought he was breaking up a meeting of the Ku Klux Klan. ❖